To deares'

On the o   next
to be a
Cathedral.

Autumn 2017 with much love
+ prayers from Alice + family x.

Divine Hospitality

DIVINE HOSPITALITY

A Christian–Muslim Conversation

Fadi Daou and Nayla Tabbara
Translated by Alan J. Amos

**World Council
of Churches**
Publications

DIVINE HOSPITALITY
A Christian–Muslim Conversation
Fadi Daou and Nayla Tabbara

Translated from the French *L'hospitalité divine. L'autre dans le dialogue des théologies chrétienne et musulmane* (LIT Verlag, 2014). English translation copyright © 2017 WCC Publications. All rights reserved. Except for brief quotations in notices or reviews, no part of this book may be reproduced in any manner without prior written permission from the publisher. Write: publications@wcc-coe.org.

WCC Publications is the book publishing programme of the World Council of Churches. Founded in 1948, the WCC promotes Christian unity in faith, witness, and service for a just and peaceful world. A global fellowship, the WCC brings together 348 Protestant, Orthodox, Anglican, and other churches representing more than 550 million Christians in 110 countries and works cooperatively with the Roman Catholic Church.

Opinions expressed in WCC Publications are those of the authors.

adyan   This research has been done in the framework of the Institute of Citizenship and Diversity Management – Aydan Foundation, Lebanon: www.adyanfoundation.org – and supported by the Institute of Missiology of Missio, Germany – www.mwi-aachen.org.

Scripture quotations are from the New Revised Standard Version Bible, © copyright 1989 by the Division of Christian Education of the National Council of the Churches of Christ in the USA. Used by permission.

Cover design: Michelle Cook / 4 Seasons Book Design
Cover image: "Abraham Receiving the Three Strangers and Sarah in the Tent." Illustration from Jami' al-Tawarikh of Rashid al-Din. Tabriz, 1314.
Book design and typesetting: Michelle Cook / 4 Seasons Book Design
ISBN: 978-2-8254-1692-1

World Council of Churches
150 route de Ferney, P.O. Box 2100
1211 Geneva 2, Switzerland
http://publications.oikoumene.org

CONTENTS

FOREWORD

Clare Amos

One of the joys and privileges for me over recent years while working in the field of interreligious engagement at the World Council of Churches has been to get to know – just a little – the two co-authors of this book, Fadi Daou and Nayla Tabbara. I will not forget hearing Fadi speak powerfully at a conference held in Beirut in 2012, presenting, in quite demanding terms, a challenge to his fellow co-religionists in the Middle East to engage with society in the region in ways that would help lead to the transformation of their nations. Nor will I forget Nayla's exquisite – that is not too strong a word – talks offered at the Bossey interreligious summer school in 2016 in which she married together a profound exploration of the theme of migration in classical Islamic sources with reflection on the implications for our world today.

That combination of scholarship, the deep rootedness of both Nayla and Fadi in their respective faiths, a willingness to look at tradition through fresh eyes and discover new insights, and an awareness of the responsibility of theology to speak into contemporary realities is also what marks out this book, which is both short and substantial. Hospitality, the theme around which the book revolves, is not an optional extra but is an image has been fundamental to the lived experience of the Middle East for many centuries, in spite of the current painful actualities of the region. Hospitality fully understood is something which changes not only those who receive it, but also those who do the offering. Divine hospitality, a theme which takes as its scriptural starting point the welcome offered by Abraham and Sarah to mysterious strangers, recounted in a story which has caught the theological and symbolic imagination of Muslims, Christians, and Jews, is what drives this book. This is so both in terms of the book's fundamental vision – of a God whose very nature demands that we expand our openness toward the other – and in terms of the methodology Fadi and Nayla have employed, which is a dialogical conversation between the two of them. Responding chapter by chapter to each other, they tread a path in which new insights are discovered.

During my years of working at the World Council of Churches, I am glad that my colleagues and I have been supported in our aim to ensure that our work of practical interreligious engagement and cooperation is underpinned by serious theological exploration of the resources that our religious tradition offers for dialogue, and the treasures that we can bring to the tent and table of meeting. We are indeed committed to practical projects and concrete outcomes for our work. But I also believe that unless accompanied by a theological seriousness which digs deep into our own faith, the work of interreligious dialogue and cooperation can fall into an undermining trap of shallowness and superficiality. So I cherish this book, in which its authors make clear their own dedication to such theological seriousness.

The work was originally published in French, then in Arabic and German, and I am glad and honoured that Fadi, Nayla, and the Adyan Foundation consented to allow the World Council of Churches to produce a translation into English, which will help this significant theological writing reach an Anglophone audience. I am grateful to Alan Amos for undertaking the translation into English as an expression of his own dedication to work for mutual understanding between Muslims and Christians in Lebanon and the Middle East. In one sense, the book needs no further validation than its own excellence. However, those of us who have had the privilege to visit the Adyan Foundation in Beirut, of which Nayla and Fadi are co-founders and its Institute of Citizenship and Diversity Management, rightly cannot help but read this book in the light of our knowledge of this ground-breaking venture. Adyan works with Christians and Muslims, especially young Christians and Muslims, in Lebanon and other Arab countries, on a variety of important projects that are intended to foster a spirit of unity in diversity in that country and that will act in turn as beacons for other parts of the world. The committed work of Fadi and Nayla in together building up the Adyan Foundation as an example of interreligious hospitality can be considered a practical outcome and expression of the spirit which shines so strongly through the pages of this book.

—Clare Amos
Programme Coordinator, Interreligious Dialogue and Cooperation
World Council of Churches

PREFACE

It is a paradox that at a time of renewal for Christian theology and the emergence of Muslim thinking which is modern and open to question from other cultures and religions, a good number of Christians and Muslims should be ruled by feelings of mistrust, even mutual hostility. "Man makes an enemy of what he is ignorant of," said Imam Ali. But mutual incomprehension is not the only reason for these negative feelings. Communal memories are laden with the conflicts and political tensions of the centuries, which are both real and symbolic factors causing alienation. To that may be added the fear and mistrust brought about by the current situation in some Muslim majority countries, where the problem of violent fundamentalism does not appear to be decreasing. And we cannot ignore the undermining of the credibility of Western society and its institutions in the eyes of many Muslims by the politics of rampant injustice. We refer above all to the Palestinian problem, but also to support given by the West to despotic and corrupt regimes that are incapable of responding to demands for justice and dignity for all, coming particularly from the new generations making use of the internet and social media.

Neither mutual encounter, nor the discovery of "the other," nor critical theology is able to deal with this problem, which has so many different ramifications. Theology, however, still retains its responsibility to offer a discourse and a reflection faithful to the principles of the faith of the two religions concerning the relationship of each with the other. Theology and religious discourse cannot be held solely responsible for intercommunal problems, yet they are not always innocent of promoting a cultural environment hostile to "otherness," particularly to the religious other.

In fact, when religious experience expresses itself primarily in terms of communal identity, faith is relegated to secondary importance, as are also the spiritual and moral values which accompany it. In such circumstances, sectarian views that draw upon religion and community identity may multiply, to the detriment of engagement with society and with others in the light of the faith. Whether you are a believer or not seems to become almost insignificant if it is a matter of defending your own community or your own religious identity. In such a situation, people are motivated by those fears, prejudices, and stereotypes which are commonly found in attitudes toward the other. This disassociation between religious belonging and faith engagement puts theology face to face with challenges to its credibility and authenticity. Believers should not be so blinded by fear that they cannot see what their own faith requires of them, including the need for a true understanding of the other. And yet at the same time, openness toward the other and the experience of encounter must not lose the spirit of critical awareness and the desire for true justice.

While theology in itself is unable to resolve the problems of Muslim–Christian relations, it remains nevertheless indispensable in guiding believers in their thinking and attitude toward those of other faiths, and in enabling true faithfulness to the will of God. Theology must not lose hope and abandon its role of critical watchfulness by colluding with human deviations of all kinds, despite the limits of its power and influence upon the political scene. And so this book hopes to offer to its readers – Christians, Muslims, and others – a clear presentation of the question of religious difference, seen from a faith perspective. In other words, our objective is to show what the Christian and Muslim faiths teach with regard to religious "otherness" and to indicate the relationship which may link the believer of another religion to God.

The following reflection is not therefore a discourse developed with the other faith always in mind, in a way that could risk a watering down of truth with the aim of securing greater sympathy and mutual acceptance. Instead, it represents a systematic theological attempt to put believers in touch with the deepest truth of their own faith. Often, in fact, the ignorance which most harms interreligious relations is ignorance of our own faith, rather than of the faith of the other. The challenge this book brings to the believer is to be willing to approach the other, not equipped with a rigid religious identity like a kind of breastplate, but with the conviction that the spiritual message the other holds is not foreign to God's plan, and that this may also be understood from the perspective of the believer's own faith.

Each one gains by discovering the theology of the other and of other religions, in Islam as in Christianity. What do the Qur'an and Muslim theology say about Christians and others? What view does the Christian have, based on his or her faith in Jesus Christ, of Muslims and of all non-Christians? What are the biblical and Qur'anic foundations for such thinking, and what are the spiritual, ethical, and practical consequences? It is to these kinds of questions that we have attempted to provide clear and well-argued responses throughout this book.

The decision to do this together has allowed us to develop a new responsive approach which we call "theologies in dialogue." In fact, this work is not a theological dialogue, where each presents straightforwardly their point of view concerning the other on the basis of their own theories and concepts and then eventually agrees to enter into the discussion of ideas. Our approach permits us, rather, to respond to the questions of the other through recourse to the inner religious tradition of our questioner. We are thus able to direct the reflection toward a shared understanding and a shared responsibility with regard to the sincerity and authenticity of spiritual experiences, and the coherence and goodness of the divine will. It is a method entirely different from one governed by polemic and apologetic on the one hand, or by compromise and syncretism on the other. We are aware of the exceptional nature of this method, and convinced of its fruitfulness. It requires the integration of the other and their questioning into the field of reflection, even the field of faith, belonging to each of the two parties to the dialogue. Instead of thinking of the other as an adversary when we encounter irreconcilable differences, the partner in dialogue is thought of as a companion on the way. For, when all is said and done, the fundamental mission of the theology of religions is to be concerned not with difference in identity but with the unity of the divine plan for the whole of creation.

This book therefore contains two theologies, the one Christian and the other Muslim. We recognize and accept the irreducible divergence in viewpoint between Christianity and Islam, in the sense that each one of these two religions lays claim to a universal interpretation of the whole of reality and of the relation between God and humanity. As a result, there is an irreconcilable divergence between the two religions, which we must respect. This does not however prevent us addressing each of the two theologies and examining them concerning the significance of the other and of religious difference.

In fact, despite their claims to universality, neither Christian nor Muslim theologies represent a closed and static system. To the extent that they seek to interpret and to transmit the truth, the two theologies are necessarily dynamic and conditioned as much by human intelligence as by their historical and cultural circumstances. This permits us to take our reflection forward, while avoiding the temptation of an absolutism which turns religion into a static image, denying reality. We recognize also the personal and contextual aspect of our reflection, even while we are addressing fundamental problems concerning both theologies.

For the theologian, the specialist in religious studies, for the student, and for the believer and every reader interested by the problem of interreligious relations and the theology of religious pluralism in Christianity and Islam, this book is aimed to be a guide, not toward final answers, but toward a way of thinking of the other, in greater faithfulness to one's own true self. For some, this reading will not be possible without a certain change of thinking and outlook. Others may be amazed at the generosity and flexibility of theological reflection, whether Christian or Muslim. Perhaps yet others may be shocked to discover the gap between those views given prominence in the media, and in society – even among leaders of thought and opinion – and the complexity, richness, and potentiality of theology in the field of plurality and of interreligious relations. Finally, we hope that for all our readers, this book will be a star which shines brightly enough to show that the darkness of obscurantism, fanaticism and terrorism can never defeat the light of truth and goodness, which we can see reflected in the faces of so many Christian and Muslim witnesses.

It is with joy that we dedicate this work, the fruit of a shared journey of research, to all our readers. We think especially of those who are seeking a deeper understanding of their faith in the light of religious diversity and the need for a shared human responsibility for our world. We hope that this book will encourage further research and publications in this field.

We wish also to thank all those who have so carefully contributed to revising our text, who have brought us greater clarity through their questions and have offered us constructive advice, particularly Mgr Guy-Paul Noujaim, Professor Adel Theodore Khoury, Professor Radwan As-Sayyid, and Professor Pierre Lory, as well as Mgr Jean-Marc Aveline, author of the foreword to the French edition of our book.

Our gratitude also is due to the Institute of Missiology – Misso (Aachen) for contributing to the financing of the research on this subject; Les Éditions Paulistes, who have published the Arabic version of the book; and l'Institut catholique de la Méditerranée for their collaboration in producing the French edition. And we are grateful to Alan Amos for his careful and insightful translation of the text into English.

—Nayla Tabbara and Fadi Daou

TRANSLATOR'S NOTE

In rendering verses from the Qur'an into English, I have referred to the Arabic text and have been guided by the translations provided by Sahih International, and those of Tarif Khalidi, A.J. Arberry, and A. Yusuf Ali.

My starting point has been the text of the Qur'anic passages in French as given in the French edition, *L'Hospitalité divine*. That has been important in providing a translation which is consistent with the interpretation of the Qur'anic verses given there by the authors. Strictly speaking, the Qur'an cannot be "translated" but the meaning can only be approximated by any translator.

So far as verses of the Bible are concerned, I have in general followed the NRSV.

In conclusion, I would also note that the nature of the religious texts limits to an extent the scope of the translator in the use of inclusive language.

—Alan J. Amos

1. CHRIST AND THE OTHER
Union Embracing Difference

Fadi Daou

For the Christian, Christ cannot just be reduced to the status of the founder of a new religion called "Christianity." Christ must be understood, in the fullness of his divine mystery, as providing the foundation for a new phase in human history. He is the new Adam, the human person restored, the author of a humanity renewed from within through his presence in the world. It follows, therefore, that while Christians acknowledge themselves as his disciples and members of his mystical body, the church, through faith, they also believe that through the free action of grace every human being is called into the saving mystery of Christ and united with him.

The Christ event – the incarnation of the eternal Word of God who dies and is raised to life – is the key by which we interpret Christianity, but it is more than that; for Christians it is the key to understanding all human existence. In order to look at the relationship between Christians and members of other religions, we have to address this fundamental reality. From the Christian perspective, even though this connection between religions has not been recognized in the history of our relationships, it has already been established through the bond which unites Christ with all humanity. Our true relationship with other religions can only be discovered through this fundamental perception that God is present in every interreligious encounter and interaction; in fact God is present in every human encounter. Christians cannot build a relationship with those of other beliefs except upon this foundation of their own relationship to God, and God's relationship to others. And so, before exploring and analyzing the way Christians understand Christ as universal saviour, we should look at how Christ understood himself, and what kind of an attitude he showed toward others, particularly toward non-Jews, and people who were not among his followers.

Interreligious Experiences of Christ

In the New Testament, the four evangelists show us Jesus as present and active mostly in the regions of Galilee and Judea. Even if during the missionary years of his life he is often on the move, the boundary of his activity corresponds to the territory where the Jewish people lived during that time. For example, there is a very clear contrast between the extent of his travels and those of the apostle Paul, who visited the whole of the East and North of the Mediterranean region.

Christ shares this limited goal with his apostles when he sends them out on mission for the first time, saying: "Go nowhere among the Gentiles, and enter no town of the Samaritans, but go rather to the lost sheep of the house of Israel" (Matt. 10:5-6). However this Judeocentric aspect of Jesus' mission contrasts strongly with his final instructions addressed to the apostles after his resurrection: "Go therefore and make disciples of all nations" (Matt. 28:19); also: "You will be my witnesses in Jerusalem, in all Judea and Samaria, and to the ends of the earth" (Acts 1:8).

Between these first and second missions came the confrontation opposing Jesus to the Jewish authorities of the time, culminating according to the account in Matthew's gospel in mutual condemnation. Jesus tells them, by means of the parable of the murderous vinedressers: "The kingdom of God will be taken away from you and given to a people that produces the fruits of the kingdom" (Matt. 21:43). The chief priests with the Jewish Sanhedrin, for their part, accuse Jesus of blasphemy and decide he deserves to be put to death (cf. Matt. 26:57-66). However, I believe that the development in Jesus' approach, and the gradual opening of his message to include a universal dimension cannot just be attributed to the obstinate rejection of his message by some of the Jews, as one might perhaps think from Paul's letter to the Romans (cf. Rom. 11:11-15). It is equally the result of the true nature of his mission and of what he gained from his occasional contacts with non-Jews. I will give three examples.

The first is the encounter with the centurion, a person from a different religion and culture yet who was attracted and open to the spiritual riches of the Jewish religion. The second example takes us to an encounter with a person from a radically different religion, the religion of the Canaanites, which for the Jewish faith was traditionally castigated as a negative and even dangerous reality. Finally, the third encounter is with the Samaritan woman, who belongs to a schismatic version of Judaism. These three encounters represent different kinds of interreligious situations, and teach us about the experience of Jesus Christ in this context, and the conclusions he reached for himself and also for his disciples.

Jesus and the Roman Centurion

When a centurion meets him and asks Jesus to heal one of his servants, Jesus responds expressing admiration for the man's faith in the presence of the crowd that gathers around. In Luke's gospel, this centurion is described as being close to the Jews, and generous toward their community (cf. Luke 7:4-5). All the same, he still represents the Roman occupation and is an outsider. According to Matthew, Jesus uses this encounter to show publicly his appreciation of the faith of a non-Jew, and yet at the same time to deliver a warning to the Jews themselves. He says, "Truly I tell you, in no one in Israel have I found such faith. I tell you, many will come from east and west and will eat with Abraham and Isaac and Jacob in the kingdom of heaven, while the heirs of the kingdom will be thrown into the outer darkness" (Matt. 8:10-12).

Here Jesus reveals a fundamental element of "his theology" of religion; his recognition of the faith of the centurion is strong and straightforward. He makes it plain that it is not ethnic or religious identity that admits people to "the kingdom" (that is, to divine grace), but the authenticity and sincerity of personal faith. He then says to the Pharisees: "Do not presume to say to yourselves, 'We have Abraham as our ancestor'; for I tell you, God is able from these stones to raise up children to Abraham" (Matt. 3:9). "If you are Abraham's children, then do what Abraham did" (John 8:39).

Jesus and the Canaanite Woman

Our second example of Jesus meeting strangers is his encounter with the Canaanite woman (cf. Matt. 15:21-28). He had come to the region of Tyre and Sidon in order to have some kind of "retreat" with his apostles, far from the crowds which followed him everywhere in Galilee. While he thought he would be unknown in a strange land, a Canaanite woman approached him and asked for healing for her daughter. Although at first Jesus tried to avoid contact with this woman, insisting harshly on his exclusive calling for mission to his own people, eventually he responded favourably, for he could not be indifferent to this woman's faith. And so, after his initial response shaped by the difference which separated them: "It is not fair to take the children's food and throw it to the dogs" (Matt. 15:26), Jesus moved on to commend the faith which he found in the Canaanite woman: "Woman, great is your faith! Let it be done for you as you wish" (Matt. 15:28). This extraordinary encounter completely overturns the presuppositions and prejudices rooted in tradition which had resulted in Jews being very distrustful, even scornful, of the Canaanites and their religion. It helped Jesus to see that difference – even religious difference – is not sufficient reason for mistrust. His own conduct shows that belonging to one or another religion is not the criterion of the authenticity and strength of a person's faith.

Jesus, therefore, does not hesitate to criticize harshly the scribes and the Pharisees, those who sit in the seat of Moses, for they offer people the appearance of being righteous, while within they are full of hypocrisy and sin (cf. Matt. 23:28). But he praises the faith of the Canaanite woman though her own religious tradition was decried as the absolute opposite or threatening alternative to the purity and integrity of Judaism. For certain commentators, this encounter represents – in the gospel of Matthew – a turning point in Jesus' understanding of his mission, which from this point expands to embrace a universal dimension.

Jesus and the Samaritan Woman

I conclude these examples with the dialogue between Christ and the Samaritan woman, as reported in the fourth chapter of John's gospel (cf. John 4:1-42). As she tries to find out his viewpoint on their religious differences, this woman gives Christ the chance to reveal his own understanding of religion. Replying to her challenge, "Our ancestors worshiped on this mountain, but you say that the place where people must worship is in Jerusalem" (John 4:20), Jesus affirms, "Woman, believe me, the hour is coming when you will worship the Father neither on this mountain nor in Jerusalem.... But the hour is coming, and is now here, when the true worshipers will worship the Father in spirit and truth" (John 4:21-23).

From this we can see that for Jesus Christ the adoration of God is not a matter of religious observance, where you know the best place in which to worship or the rules laid down by local culture as to how you must practice your religion. Rather, Jesus places worship at the highest level, where authenticity of faith and spiritual communion with God count above all else.

We find here certainly a "relativization" of religious practices and even of beliefs, but this does not mean the abolition of these, but rather giving priority to inner spiritual experience. Instead of pronouncing on the choice between the Jewish religion and that of the Samaritans,[1] Jesus puts forward a new approach. He provides a unique interpretation of religion that he calls all the world to follow. He teaches that it is not the diversity of understandings which creates a problem, but the superficiality of religious practices and theological debates which reflect the intrigues and selfish interests of human beings rather than to the will of God. In his response to the Samaritan woman, Jesus Christ invites us to an encounter with God, not on such or such a mountain, or according to such or such an observance, but in himself, in the heart of his interior life and in the truth of his own being.

Faith, the Way to Union in Love

Christ's understanding of faith

The attitude of Jesus as he encounters people of other religious backgrounds provides us with three elements on which to reflect. First, Jesus is far from embracing a communitarian logic which would install a rigid separation between our own community and that of others. His attitude refutes and rejects a binary vision of the world that defines people as belonging to two separate groups: the believers on the one side, and the unbelievers on the other. The attention that he gives to the people whom he meets is free from feelings of mistrust or hostility which can arise from rejection and conscious or unconscious fear of the other. Ethnic or religious difference does not prevent him from being aware of the spiritual experience of each person in its originality and authenticity.

Second, we find with Jesus a recognition and admiration of the faith of those who are neither Jews nor his disciples. So, when Christ admires the faith of the centurion or of the Canaanite woman, he sees that God is at work in the life of people of all cultures and religions. Perhaps some may think when looking at these examples that the faith of these people was actually faith in the person of Jesus Christ and his divine power. Certainly this could be true. Nevertheless, the reaction of Jesus shows admiration for the trust these people have in God and his mercy, and this leads him to grant their request for transformation and healing. Beyond questions of religious identity, the encounter with Christ reveals the importance of an authentic relationship uniting the human person to God, regardless of the diversity of religious practices. Christians may, for their part, interpret the faith of others as being inwardly and implicitly guided by Christ, the Word of God, who, coming into the world, enlightens every human being (cf. John 1:9). Even so, they may not deny the existence of the gift of faith to others, even though these do not express it in Christian terminology.

Finally, it is clear that Christ emphasizes the importance of the interior dimension of the faith and experience of each person rather than outward observances. It is sincere relationship with God and the commitment that flows from this which counts, rather than vain disputes with a view to a supposed religious purity or a righteousness based on observances, which ends by transforming religion into empty and self-regarding appearances. And so the attitude of Jesus Christ toward persons of other religions may find its echo in this word of the apostle Peter: "I truly understand that God shows no partiality, but in every nation anyone who fears him and does what is right is acceptable to him" (Acts 10:34-35).

Some may challenge this understanding of the relation of Jesus to people of another faith by referring to verses or passages from the Bible that display a more exclusive dimension of the Christian faith. Certainly, Jesus often gave teaching marked by a radicalism that created separation, sometimes even within the same household. He proclaims: "Do not think that I have come to bring peace to the earth; I have not come to bring peace, but a sword. For I have come to set a man against his father, and a daughter against her mother, and a daughter-in-law against her mother-in-law; and one's foes will be members of one's own household" (Matt.10:34-36). Jesus explains this sentence in terms of the total detachment required of those who commit to following him. Each disciple is called to carry his or her cross, following the example of Christ, the sign of universal love and self-offering.

In response to someone's question about the number of those who will be saved, Jesus replies that salvation will be offered to those who strive to enter "by the narrow gate." But even though it seems a paradox, Jesus makes it plain that those who have followed him will fare no better than "the others." For the first may hear on judgment day, "I do not know where you come from; go away from me, all you evildoers!" (Luke 13:27); while others will come "from east and west, from north and south, and will eat in the kingdom of God" (Luke 13:29). So it will be that "some are last who will be first, and some are first who will be last" (Luke 13:30).

To sum up, the radical nature of the gospel message is quite evident, and allows no one to believe that the way of salvation is easy and plain sailing. And yet the strongest demands are made on the followers of Christ, while at the same time the door of salvation is left open to others. It is very clear that just having a religious affiliation is no visa for heaven, and that surprises about the allocation of places in heaven are to be expected. At every opportunity Jesus reminds his followers that in his Father's house, there are many rooms (cf. John 14:2).

Despite the fact that the church in the course of its history has sometimes interpreted the radical gospel message too narrowly – we may recall the statement "outside the church, there is no salvation"[2] – the interreligious experiences of Jesus given above must remain our guide. These gospel accounts show that when Jesus encountered others he did so with a sensitive and sincere attention to their needs and to their religious and spiritual experiences. In fact, Christ does not reject in principle any religion, but he criticizes vehemently religious hypocrisy that shows itself in legalistic formalism, and an exterior observance stripped of spirituality and sincere ethical engagement (cf. Matt. 23:1-36).

Above all, the gospels clearly witness to the fact that Jesus Christ considers himself the bearer of a unique and universal message of salvation. From this comes the mission command he gives to his apostles: "Go therefore and make disciples of all nations, baptizing them in the name of the Father and of the Son and of the Holy Spirit, and teaching them to obey everything that I have commanded you. And remember, I am with you always, to the end of the age" (Matt. 28:19-20).

The apostles have indeed carried forward the message of their master with its double dynamic of oneness and universality. Paul expresses this well in his letter to Timothy, writing: "God our Saviour ... desires everyone to be saved and to come to the knowledge of the truth. For there is one God; there is also one mediator between God and humankind, Christ Jesus, himself human, who gave himself a ransom for all" (1 Tim. 2:3-6). I will return later to the implications of this teaching for the recognition of other religions by Christianity, as well as the understanding of mission.

This dual reality of universality and oneness in the person and teaching of Christ is necessary both for faithfulness to the Christian message in its global witness and for its coherence. At the same time, this book does not seek in any way to obscure anything that does not suit its argument in order to show only evidence that supports an opening toward and a ready acceptance of religious plurality. While respecting the principle of the interrelatedness of every religion within the diverse and global spiritual experience of humanity, I seek to show here the hospitality of God acting upon the particular interior understanding and very conception of the Christian faith. And so after having seen the approach adopted by Jesus toward others, and before looking at the theological consequences of the Christ event for the view which Christians hold with regard to others, I wish to focus on the content of the message that Christ has sought to transmit and that his disciples have presented in the gospels.

The universality of the spirituality of the gospels

Blessed are the poor in spirit, for theirs is the kingdom of heaven.
Blessed are those who mourn, for they will be comforted.
Blessed are the meek, for they will inherit the earth.
Blessed are those who hunger and thirst for righteousness, for they will be filled.

Blessed are the merciful, for they will receive mercy.

Blessed are the pure in heart, for they will see God.

Blessed are the peacemakers, for they will be called children of God.

Blessed are those who are persecuted for righteousness' sake, for theirs is the kingdom of heaven. (Matt. 5:3–10)

This passage of the gospel, known as the Beatitudes, represents the heart of the message of Jesus Christ. Here we find in condensed form both the originality of the gospel message and the universality of human spiritual experience. As a result, this text has become a sort of universal spiritual resource in which people of different religious traditions find themselves at home, as it expresses a dimension of their own spiritual path.

In reality, the Sermon on the Mount, of which the Beatitudes form the kernel, is a teaching that Jesus has delivered as a testament for his disciples as well as for the whole of humanity. The importance of this passage is that it is not purely theoretical teaching but rather a picture that shows us how Christ himself has lived, and how those may live who accept the call of God to abandon a life centred egotistically on themselves, opening themselves instead to a life centred on the love of God and of others.

St John in his first epistle translates this message into words as simple as they are beautiful. He reminds us first of all that the life to which we are called is founded on the divine choice to love us freely and completely. "In this is love, not that we loved God but that he loved us and sent his Son to be the atoning sacrifice for our sins" (1 John 4:10). From which follows the appeal: "Beloved, let us love one another, because love is from God; everyone who loves is born of God and knows God. Whoever does not love does not know God, for God is love" (1 John 4:7-8).

This message has a double impact. First, it constitutes a measure of the authenticity of the faith of those who call themselves Christian. "Whoever does not love abides in death," says St John (1 John 3:14).

And so to be Christian means to follow Christ on the path of love, a universal love which expresses itself not only in words but in deeds and in truth, even in the love of the enemy. Christians cannot therefore consider their relation to people of other religious traditions except on the basis of this interior attitude, as fundamental as it is unconditional.

Second, the gospel message throws open the boundaries of the Christian community and carries forward a truth – from the point of view of Christian faith – that is addressed to the whole of humanity. Truly, the love of God is a love that is universal and free. It does not depend on any predisposition or human response. Christians believe that every human person is enlightened by Christ, who has given his life for all: "No one has greater love than this, to lay down one's life for one's friends" (John 15:13).

In a study on the Bible and believers from other religions, Sri Lankan pastor Wesley Ariarajah concludes that the biblical message insists above all on the priority of grace and on God's acceptance of us rather than on our own acceptance of God. "The people whom we meet," he writes, "no matter from what race, age or religion, are children of God. And this conviction that the other is truly a child of God in exactly the same way as you and me, this must be the basis of all dialogue with our neighbours."[3] God loves all human beings and considers them his children. Through his only Son, he makes us all his "adopted children." But can that be true for those who have not explicitly recognized Jesus Christ as the incarnate Word of God, put to death and raised up for the salvation of the world?

The human person, dwelling place of God

Christ has a clear vision of his own person, and of his mission. He declares: "I am the way, and the truth, and the life. No one comes to the Father except through me"(John 14:6). Furthermore, his relation-ship to the Father is unique and is founded on a unity within the very being of God. So, at the request of Philip, one of his apostles, "Lord, show us the Father and we will be satisfied" (John 14:8), Jesus replies: "'Have I been with you all this time, Philip, and you still do not know me? Whoever has seen me has seen the Father" (John 14:9). And Jesus continues: "Believe me that I am in the Father and the Father is in me" (John 14:11). It is these words, among others, that enable John, in the beginning of his gospel, to affirm at one and the same time the unity of the divine being and the divinity of Jesus Christ, as he writes: "In the beginning was the Word,[4] and the Word was with God, and the Word was God" (John 1:1).

How may one reconcile a message of universal love with a theological affirmation which is so very particular? It is impossible to respond to this enigmatic question without considering the two dimensions of the mission of Jesus Christ. By the fact that he is the eternal Word of God, by whom all has been made, Christ is the foundation of the existence of every human being and is a stranger to no one. By his incarnation and his gift of himself through love for all, he is also a source of grace for all humankind. Further, beyond this universal dimension of his person and of his mission, Jesus Christ is, for those who believe in him and his word, a source of special grace so extraordinary that it turns upside down the logic of things and makes of the human person the host of God. Jesus teaches: "Those who love me will keep my word, and my Father will love them, and we will come to them and make our home with them" (John 14:23).

We can therefore say that the summit of divine hospitality is achieved by God coming to seek a place for himself in the heart of the human person whom he loves. The special calling of the Christian faith is to welcome this, and to invite others to this shared mutual indwelling and union between the human and the divine, which reflects the pattern of the perfect union of the two natures human and divine in the person of Jesus Christ. We must never forget that the ground of this union is love. St John recalls this very clearly in his epistle: "God is love, and those who abide in love abide in God, and God abides in them" (1 John 4:16). This proclaims the universality of the gift of union with God through Christ, and opens this possibility to those who do not confess the Christian faith.

As a result, we may speak of two forms of union between God and humanity. The first is an explicit union, in which a human being recognizes Christ, the eternal Word of God, through whom the union of humanity with the divine nature is achieved. Such a person lives out this union through sharing in the sacramental life of the church and by means of the sacrament of universal human solidarity in the context of the world around.

There is also a second form of union, which I call implicit, and which, like the first, is founded on the initiative of divine grace and applies to all those who do not recognize in the same way as Christians the Lordship of Christ. In this instance, we suggest that this union is accomplished and sustained through the mystery of the free gift of God's love.

In the parable of the last judgment in Matthew's gospel, Christ addresses those who are righteous, saying,

> Come, you that are blessed by my Father, inherit the kingdom pre-pared for you from the foundation of the world; for I was hungry and you gave me food, I was thirsty and you gave me something to drink.... Then the righteous will answer him, "Lord, when was it that we saw you hungry and gave you food, or thirsty and gave you something to drink?" ... And the king will answer them, "Truly I tell you, just as you did it to one of the least of these who are members of my family, you did it to me." (See: Matt. 25:31-46)

These righteous ones whom Christ calls "you that are blessed by my Father" are people from all nations and religions. Because they act prompted by love alone, without any calculation or hope of reward, they are drawn into this mystery of the implicit union that Christ achieves between God and humanity.

A question remains, does the religion of these persons share in the fulfilment of this union with God, as Christianity does by means of the sacramental life? Or is this union of non-Christians with God through Christ accomplished apart from or even despite the context of their own particular religious experience? Later on, when I come to speak of the Christian position on religious plurality, I will tackle these questions. For the moment, in the context of this chapter on the personal relationship of Christ with all people, I would like to conclude my thoughts by showing how, from the perspective of Christian theology, the grace of the incarnate Christ and the paschal mystery has an effect upon non-Christians.

Humanity made new in Christ

Thanks to the mystery of the incarnation, which signifies a total union between divinity and humanity in the person of Jesus Christ, the church has a particular vision of human nature, for we are called ourselves to enter into this divine communion. The church fathers expressed this by saying "the Son of God became human, so that humans might become children of God."[5] So by the revelation of God in a human person, according to the Second Vatican Council, human beings "through Christ the Word made flesh, partake in the Holy Spirit of one being with the Father, and are made participants of the divine nature" (*Dei Verbum: Constitution on Divine Revelation*, section 2.). Christian de Chergé[6] eloquently interprets this fundamental truth of the mystery of Christ, saying, "The primary meaning of 'the Incarnation' is not that the Word becomes flesh, but that our flesh should be taken into the divine life *[le milieu divin]*."[7]

The Catholic Church has clarified the meaning of this fundamental change brought about by Christ in the life of each human person in one of the most beautiful pages of the writings from the Second Vatican Council. My reflection which follows is, therefore, based on section 22 of the Pastoral Constitution *Gaudium et spes*. In the light of Christ, this text puts the human person at the heart of the whole universal history of salvation. "The other," whether Muslim, Jew, or nonbeliever, is thus for the Christian the bearer of a grace originating from Christ, often not at the conscious level, but nevertheless effective.

The union of Christ with all humanity

The point of departure for Christian anthropology is surely the *imago Dei*: human beings created by God in God's own image and according to God's own likeness (cf. Gen. 1:26). This reality is nevertheless to be interpreted in the light of Christ. Adam was in reality the type of the one who was to come, Jesus Christ, who will be called the new Adam and who "fully reveals humanity to itself and brings to light its very high calling" (*Gaudium et spes* 22.1).

This conciliar text locates the foundation of our human dignity in the double victory of Jesus Christ over sin and death. The church considers that the divine likeness in human beings has been marred by sin and is therefore in need of being restored. Truly, the burden of suffering and death would be completely crushing for human beings if this condition were not to be given a new meaning, and transfigured by the grace of new life. Christians believe that, by their binding to Christ, they become conformed to his image and share in his victory over death, thanks to the paschal mystery and the action of the Holy Spirit, which enable them to partake already in the life of the resurrection (cf. *Gaudium et spes* 22.4). What then is Christ for the non-Christian?

The Council is clear on this point, establishing the foundations of Christian anthropology and of all Christian thinking concerning the other. The raising of human nature to a stature without equal, by the very fact that the eternal Word of God has fully assumed this nature, is, for Christians, a reality with universal significance. To put this in other words, "by his incarnation, he, the Son of God has in a certain way united himself with each individual. He worked with human hands, thought with a human mind. He acted with a human will, and with a human heart he loved" (*Gaudium et spes* 22.2).

The very fact of the incarnation constitutes therefore a kind of new creation, in which human nature itself receives a new dimension. From then on, all human beings, independently both of their own religious allegiance and of Christianity, are in relationship with Christ, because Christ Jesus is himself united to them.

The universal dynamic of the paschal mystery

This union of Christ with each human person obliges Christians to regard themselves and others with respect, even reverence. Furthermore, the other is not just raised in stature by the union of Christ with human nature, but also linked into the mystery of salvation, which renews humanity from within and opens for all humankind the gate to life and eternal bliss (cf. the Council's *Lumen gentium*: *Constitution on the Church*, 16). Speaking of the way in which the believer enters into the paschal mystery, the conciliar text puts this as follows: "All this holds true not only for Christians but for all people of good will, in whose heart grace is active invisibly" (*Gaudium et spes* 22.5). And the Council adds: "For since Christ died for everyone and since all are in fact called to one and the same destiny, we must hold that the Holy Spirit offers to all the possibility of being made partners, in a way known to God, in the paschal mystery (*Gaudium et spes* 22.5).

United with Christ and associated with his paschal mystery, by grace and according to the generosity and mysterious will of God, every human being is therefore included in the universal covenant accomplished by Jesus Christ. Such is then the stature and greatness of the mystery of the human person with regard to Christians, a mystery which is fundamentally associated with that of Christ. Also every human being is by grace a "Christ-like being." But this profound reality with regard to human persons can only be perceived with the eyes of faith, or according to the Father's own vision. In his spiritual testament, Christian de Chergé sees his death as an opportunity to bring this vision into focus, and also this joy which allows him to see the transfiguration at work in the life of his friends, the Muslims. He says: "Here it is that I am able, if God so pleases, to steep my own vision in that of the Father in order to contemplate his children of Islam, wholly illuminated by the glory of Christ, fruits of his Passion, clothed in the gift of the Spirit, whose secret joy will always be to establish communion and to re-establish the likeness, while overcoming differences."[8]

The Christian Viewpoint

Two criticisms can be raised here. The first will accuse this approach of an inclusivism which consists in defining the good that one sees in others by using criteria which apply within Christianity. To appreciate the religious and spiritual wealth of others only in the measure where one is able to assimilate this to our Christian experience or associate this with the mystery of Christ does not satisfy my present theological enquiry. Also, I would ask the reader to have the patience to go further in reading this book in order to gain greater clarity in dealing with this question.

Nevertheless, I will add here two comments. First of all, the attitude of Jesus Christ toward others, outlined above, is larger than an inclusivist approach to religious diversity, and it represents a respect and admiration for the faith of others in its own right. Second, to speak of the universal effects of the grace of the two mysteries of the incarnation and redemption indicates note a patronizing or condescending approach on the part of the Christian toward people of other religious traditions, but on the contrary a recognition of the non-exclusivity of the mystery of Christ. This is more important for the Christian than for others. That is to say that Christians aware of this teaching cannot justify an attitude of religious discrimination toward others, for they realize that they are united with them by the one who is the centre and fundamental meaning of their lives: the Christ. To sum up, it is the transformation of the Christian, and of the view Christians have of others, that applies here, not the definition of the status of the religion of the other.

The second criticism or qualification is caused by the fact that this approach is inherently of relevance to the missionary dynamic of our faith. To believe in this union with Christ of all human beings must surely prompt Christians to reveal this truth to others and, in consequence, to invite them to recognize this grace, indeed real but unknown to them? This Christian anthropology therefore constitutes at one and the same time not only the basis of respect for the other but also a motivation for evangelization and the proclamation of Christ as universal saviour. Further on, I will take some space to analyze this question. But I want at this point to note that, thanks to this "theology of the other" in relationship to Christ, one may no longer start from "zero" in interreligious relations. Before even considering this relationship to others or starting a dialogue, we must be aware that we are already together on the way with, toward, and in God.

Encounter or dialogue must therefore take place in this spirit, rich in meaning and alive with potentiality. It is a question of observing, and of seeking to meditate together on the shared part of the route which God has brought about for us, so as to face better the part which remains for us to travel in a diversity of journeyings, but in unity with regard to our goal. In his apostolic exhortation "A New Hope for Lebanon," Pope John Paul II wrote:

> From the point of view of faith and of charity, to go toward the other cannot be limited to communicating to him that which we ourselves have understood from the Lord, but consists also in receiving from him the treasure and the truth which he has already given to be discovered. We will go forward in this way in an ever greater knowledge of the one true God and of the One whom he has sent, his Son Jesus Christ (cf. John 17:3). For if "grace and truth are come [to us] by Jesus Christ" (John 1:17), the Spirit of God, which breathes in the Church, breathes also in the human community in its totality.

2. THE ECONOMY OF THE REMINDER
Islamic Perception of the History of Revelation

Nayla Tabbara

Verses of the Qur'an that refer to "the other" are certainly numerous. However, these verses vary considerably in tone, and sometimes contradict one another. In fact, sometimes we find verses which praise "the other," notably the Christian and the Jew, and sometimes verses which instruct Muslims not to take these as allies, or verses even advocating fighting or subjugating them. At a higher level, other verses are concerned with the unity of the human race, the dignity and responsibility imparted to all human beings by God, and a calling to be open toward one another. Either treated separately and compartmentalized, or one group of verses taken to the exclusion of the other, these verses have given birth to two opposing theologies: the first perceives "the other" – meaning here the one who professes another religion – as a rival, and the second sees the other as a sibling. When treated together and as of equal weight, these verses give rise to theologies which are intrinsically contradictory and which argue simultaneously for the spirit of tolerance inherent in Islam and for the necessity of subjugating the other within a "Muslim society" or a Muslim state.

In order to infer from the Qur'an a theology of the other, which is at the same time comprehensible and coherent, it is necessary not just to take into consideration all the "positive" and the "negative" verses which deal with the other but to set them out according to a system which unifies and classifies them. Yet to begin with a contextual analysis would only lead us to error, for such an analysis would have to base itself on a shifting historical context continually subject to adaptation during the 23 years of the prophetic mission and the Qur'anic revelation. The contextual has to be evaluated in the light of the universal, so that it can be included within an overall picture which enables us to see its proper value. For this reason, in this theological sketch I begin with a panoramic view, which gradually moves from the universal and immutable to the contextual with all its upheavals and particular nuances.

The Archetypal Covenants

Two principles underpin the universal relationship of humanity with God in the Qur'an: the search for God and the preservation of an internal equilibrium or sense of balance which governs the conduct of human beings and their relationship with all that surrounds them. According to Qur'anic theology, these two principles are embedded in humanity since the time of our creation, and even before.

Humanity's initial yes

The history of the relationship between humanity and God begins, according to the Qur'an, with the word: a word of address and a word of response. The Qur'an puts forward the description of a remarkable event, an event which seals the covenant between human beings and God. This event has taken place before the existence of humankind on the earth, in what one might call a proto-existence.

The Qur'an seems to indicate that all human beings, before appearing on earth, exist in a certain form as essences. These essences have not been created in synchronicity with their successive appearance on earth, but together, simultaneously, before creation itself. They take their appointed form as they are joined with their bodies when they appear on earth, at the time of the manifestation of each essence.

It is in this other world, this "elsewhere and before," that God spoke to all human beings, to all the descendants of Adam, for the first time: "And [mention] when your Lord took from the children of Adam – from their loins – their descendants and made them testify of themselves, [saying to them], "Am I not your Lord?" (*Al A'raf* 7.172a). Upon hearing God addressing them, these essences were summoned to consciousness. They became aware of themselves at the same moment as they became aware of their Creator. And they all responded in unison: "Yes, we have testified" (*Al A'raf* 7.172b).

Every human being has therefore taken part in this yes. If God has given to human beings the blessing of breathing into them his Spirit – "Then he has formed him harmoniously and he has breathed into him of his Spirit" (*As-Sajda* 32.9) – and has honoured human beings by giving them equal dignity – "And We have certainly honoured the children of Adam and carried them on the land and sea and provided for them of the good things and preferred them over much of what We have created, with [definite] preference" (*Al Isra'* 17.70) – then it is upon this initial yes, in which all human beings have taken part, that the relationship between humanity and God is founded, a yes which is also called " primordial covenant."

Further, theologians have identified this moment of primordial testimony with the *fitra*, the "original conception or pre-disposition" – a term which means in the Qur'an the act of creation and which incorporates an innate monotheism that belongs to all human beings. So according to the *hadith*: "Every human being is born according to the *fitra*." The call to rediscover this *fitra* appears clearly in verse 30 of the *surah Ar-Rum* (30): "Submit yourself therefore humbly to the Religion, as a pure believer, according to the *fitra* (original predisposition) which God has given to human beings in creating them." Human beings are, therefore, according to their original predisposition, believing and monotheist. In addition, according to the sufi scholar Tirmidhi (3rd century AH / 9th century CE), this *fitra* is none other than the divine anointing (*sibgha*),[1] in virtue of which God has plunged all the entities (or essences) in the water of mercy. According to this interpretation, every human being is, in essence, "mercied," i.e., touched by mercy."[2]

The human yes to responsibility

Yet human beings did not stop with the first yes. From the beginnings of their history with God and of their recognition of the Lordship of God, they carry out voluntarily a task which God offers to all creation: "We have, in truth, proposed responsibility for the sacred trust (*amana*) to the heavens, to the earth, and to the mountains, but they have refused to take on this responsibility; they have been afraid of it, and it is humankind who has accepted the responsibility"(*Al Ahzab* 33.72).

This sacred trust, in Arabic *amana,* is understood differently by various Muslim exegetes and scholars. Some see here stewardship over humanity, the earth, and created order; others see the protection of the primordial covenant. I prefer to give a threefold meaning to this trust, seeing it as comprising responsibility, conscience, and a sense of balance, as will be suggested further on in this chapter.

The whole of humanity, according to the Qur'an, has therefore borne witness to the oneness of God and has taken upon itself the trust conferred by God. And so, in order to seal this agreement that human beings should take responsibility for this trust, which follows on from the first covenant, God installs humanity as God's steward or vicegerent (*khalifa*) on earth.

In an archetypal description of this appointment, the Qur'an depicts a scene which sets face to face the initial yes of humanity and the initial no of the evil one:

> When your Lord said to the angels, "I am going to set in place a steward on earth," they said: "Are you going to set in place someone who will sow corruption, and will shed blood, when we are the ones

who are celebrating Your praises, and glorifying You and sanctifying You?" The Lord said, "I know what you know not." He taught to Adam the names of all creatures, and then he showed them to the angels, saying: "Let me know their names, if you are truthful." They say "Glory to You! We only know that which You have made us know; You are, truly, the Omniscient and the Wise." He says: "O Adam! Teach them the names of these creatures!" When Adam had instructed the angels, the Lord said: "Have I not declared to you that I know the mystery of the heavens and of the earth? I know what you reveal and I know what you conceal." Then We said to the angels: "Prostrate yourselves before Adam!" They prostrated themselves with the exception of Iblis[3] who refused and puffed himself up with pride: he was one of the number of evildoers. (*Al Baqara* 2.30-34)

The *surah Al A'raf* (7) continues the story with a dialogue between God and Satan:

Yes, We have created you, then We have shaped you, then We have said to the angels: "Prostrate yourselves before Adam!" They prostrated themselves, with the exception of Iblis who did not prostrate himself. God said "What hinders you from prostrating yourself when I have commanded you to do so?" He replied: "I am better than him. You have created me out of fire, and him you have created from clay." (*Al A'raf* 7.11-12)

For all the commentators of the Qur'an, this 'no' of Satan indicates his pride and vanity. From this they infer that every human being who shows evidence of pride and arrogance is in effect following Satan. In other words, such people turn themselves into idols, associating the adoration of themselves with the adoration of God and losing their sense of balance. Pride, vanity, presumption, or arrogance are therefore the "anti-values" par excellence, and their very presence in the heart of a person succeeds in breaking the two covenants with one blow: the covenant to have none but God as Lord and the covenant of steward-ship over the earth demonstrated by equity and just balance. Thus the Qur'an insists on reminding us, by means of the instructions which the sage Luqman gives to his son, that God does not love the proud: "And do not turn your face away from people, and do not despoil the earth with arrogance: for God does not love the presumptuous who are full of vainglory"(*Luqman* 31:18). A *hadith* even goes as far as to say: "Anyone possessing just one atom of pride shall not enter para-dise." It follows that true stewardship has to be full of humility and show itself in service.

Therefore, the proto-history of humanity with God is marked by two archetypal covenants, the second following on from the first; on the one hand an implicit covenant of faithfulness to the Lord and wit-nessing to God's oneness, and in not associating any idol with God, and on the other hand a covenant to fulfil the trust and title of being steward on the earth without behaving arrogantly, but remaining always humble before God.

Revelation and the Balance

Once they have come to exist in this world of multiplicity, human beings need to be reminded of their original predisposition (*fitra*) and of the covenants made with them, which are an alliance contracted between them and God. Divine providence ensures that through their particular histories and personal relation with God, all human beings constantly receive individual reminders. These reminders may take many forms: wishes granted, favours given, or trials bringing people to face their inner depths. These reminders can also come from others who, through their example and witness, lead people to remember the divine presence and mercy. Within the collective human history, it is revelation which plays the part of this reminder.

General reminders

While the Qur'an describes how Adam has broken God's commandment, Islamic theology does not include the idea of original sin. This is because Adam quickly repented, and because God has accepted his repentance.[4] Thus Islam does not describe the action of God in history and revelation as an economy of salvation, but rather as an economy of reminder. God is therefore seen in Muslim theology as offering to human beings, both in general and in particular, occasions to remind them of their initial covenants, so that they may be mindful of him, find him once again and find also themselves, in recovering their *fitra*.

With regard to general reminders, God accompanies human beings from Adam onwards, sending prophets, chosen from among them, in order to remind them of their original testimony and in order to encourage them to renew this. Describing this succession of reminders, the Qur'an – which names itself Reminder (*dhikr*)[5] – says:

> We have sent to you a revelation as we have sent a revelation to Noah and to the prophets after him. We have sent a revelation to Abraham, Ishmael, Isaac, Jacob, to the tribes, to Jesus, to Job, to Jonah, to Aaron, to Solomon and we have given the Book of Psalms to David. [We have also sent a revelation to] messengers of whom we have spoken, and messengers whose story We have not told you. And God has spoken to Moses in a plain language. We have sent messengers proclaiming and warning, so that after the coming of these messengers there is no cause for people to argue before God. (*An-Nisa'* 4.163-165)

Also, the Qur'an insists on the fact that God has sent messengers to every people, at one time or another: "There does not exist any community where there has not been one who warns" (*Fatir* 35.24). Some of these messengers are easily recognizable, notably in the Jewish and Christian traditions, others are from among pre-Islamic Arab prophets, such as Hud and Saleh, and others open to interpretation, such as Dhul Kifl, who represents Ezekiel for the majority of Qur'anic exegetes but who indicates Buddha according to the great polymath and student of Indian culture and religion Biruni (d. 440 AH/1048 CE). The verse adds that there exist messengers "whose story We have not told you," that is to say that they are neither mentioned in the Qur'an nor in the tradition (*hadith*). This opens a wide margin for the consideration of religions not mentioned in the Qur'an but playing a part in this economy of reminder, provided they are equipped with the second criterion besides the quest for God: the Balance.

The Balance

A reading of the Qur'anic *surahs* and verses according to their chronological order, which differs from the actual order of the Qur'an,[6] enables us to take up the two essential points in Muhammad's prophetic mission: first, an appeal or reminder for the worship of the unique God, without having recourse to intermediate divinities, and for belief in the mercy and power of God above all things; secondly, a reminder of the basis of an ethical measure that ought to regulate human relations, which the Qur'an calls the Balance. Just like the primordial covenant, the Balance precedes history, as the Qur'an says: "He has raised the sky and he has established the Balance so that you do not make mistakes with the weights. Do not err concerning the balance, weigh justly and do not tamper with the balance" (*Ar-Rahman* 55.7-9).

However, throughout the history and the economy of reminder, the Balance is associated with revelation: "We have sent Our messengers with evident proofs. We have sent down with them the Book and the Balance so that human beings may practice equity" (*Al Hadid* 57.25); or again, "God is He who has sent down the Book with the Truth, as also the Balance" (*Ash-Shura* 42.17).

Thus this Balance "descends" with the revelation or with successive revelations. The Prophet Muhammed is not the first to appeal to it, but he repeats the reminders of his fellow prophets and predecessors, such as this appeal of Shu'ayb, the biblical Jethro: "Give full measure and do not be one of those who sell short; weigh with a just balance [=

correct scales.] Do not cause damage to the property of another, and do not spread corruption upon the earth" (*Ash-Shu'ara'* 26.181-183).

In effect, as it appears from the verses mentioned above, the Balance concerns justice in every relationship and transaction with others, above all when it concerns the oppressed or those who have no voice:

> Do not touch the property of the orphan, except in order to make it profitable, until such a one attains puberty. Give good measure and use just weights. – We only demand of a soul what It is able to bear – When you negotiate, be just, even if it is with a close relative. Be faithful to the covenant with God. You find there what He has commanded. Even so examine yourselves! Such is My way. It is straight; so follow it! (*Al-An'am* 6.152-153)

To keep the Balance is therefore to protect the property and the rights of others against every form of oppression, exploitation, and transgression, and to respect what is due to each person. What is more, those who are reminded of the Balance are not only expected to be careful to be just, which corresponds to the letter of the law, but to retrieve from within themselves the innate measure of justice, that is equity, which corresponds to the spirit of the law. "O believers! Be righteous before God, witnesses of equity. Do not let hatred of others cause you to be unjust. Practice equity: that is most close to piety" (*Al Ma'ida* 5.8); "If you judge, then, judge between them with equity. God loves the just" (*Al Ma'ida* 5.42); "Reconcile one with another with justice, and be equitable, for God loves the just" (*Al Hujarat* 49.9).

The Balance is therefore both a measure and a conscience, or a conscientious sense of appraisal. And this appraisal must be the same in relation to all people, whether they are close relatives or strangers, and whatever their nationality or religious affiliation. God having given dignity to each human being[7] and all human beings being equal,[8] each person must treat others with the same measure of respect. Furthermore, since human beings are considered by God as one soul – "He has created you and will raise you again as one soul" (*Luqman*

31.28) – each must treat their neighbour, whoever they may be, as if they are dealing with themselves. As the *hadith* affirms: "No-one is a believer if they do not love their neighbour as they love themselves." Thus the Balance requires equity and reciprocity, its antithesis being the application of double standards: "Woe to those who give short measure, those who, when they are served by others, demand full measure, but when they weigh or measure for others, cause them a loss!" (*Al Mutaffifin* 83.1-3).

This duty of just measure, or equity, corresponds to the trust which humanity has voluntarily accepted to honour and protect. This trust also relates to the earth and how we treat it.[9] God, through his economy of the Reminder, sends occasions, both collective and personal, in order to remind human beings of the archetypal covenant which governs our relationship with God, with our fellow human beings, with ourselves, and with the world. This fourfold relationship is summed up in the Qur'an by the expression "faith and doing good deeds." It is also referred to in numerous verses, in the more explicit form: "belief in God, belief in the last day, and doing good." Belief in the last day recalls two fundamentals of the faith: human responsibility, and the final meeting with God. The belief in the last day establishes the connection between doing good deeds, preserving the balance, and the desire to encounter God, which has remained in human beings since the time when first was heard "Am I not your Lord?" when they were but essences.

Two principles, the testimony to the oneness of God and the application of the Balance, thus underpin the relationship between humanity and God. In parallel, there are also two divine promises for each person who strives to reach them, whatever their religious affiliation, provided they keep these promises in mind: a promise of meeting God for every human being who is searching for him: "You who are striving without ceasing toward your Lord, you will meet Him"(*Al Inshiqaq* 84.6), and a promise of recognition to every person who works and shows proof of effort: "Human beings will obtain the fruit of their work, and their efforts shall be rewarded" (*An Najm* 53.39-40).

The Abrahamic Way

The two ways to God

Two ways are offered to human beings to find God once again after their creation upon earth, one by a providential re-awakening of their *fitra*, the desire for the divine placed in humanity from the time of its "original conception," as discussed above, without the need for intermediary revelation; the other by means of revelation that allows human beings, by following religion, to recover their *fitra*. To recover their *fitra* by following religion means to climb the rope provided by religious observance toward faith, or, according to Muslim terminology, to pass from *islam* (submission), toward *iman* (faith), toward *ihsan* (benevolence), which consists in adoring God as if one sees him.[10] In this case, as also in the case of the providential re-awakening of the *fitra*, it is not God who unveils Godself to human beings after having been veiled from them, but it is the human person who lifts the veils covering their conscience, in order to find once more the memory of the primordial covenant. Lebanese sociologist S. Al Mawla points out:

> In the Qur'anic discourse, impiety, non-belief, and unfaithfulness do not relate to the corruption of the will, but rather to the poor functioning of the reason. Here is unveiled the true Islamic perspective. In Islam it is the human being who hides, veiled, from God. It is not the divine who is hidden from us, but it is we ourselves who are hidden by the veils of negligence and forgetfulness, and it is for us to remove the veil and to strive to know God.[11]

The remarkable novel by the philosopher Ibn Tufail (d. 580 AH/1185 CE) entitled *Hayy Ibn Yaqzan*,[12] takes a look at these two ways through the example of three men: Hayy ibn Yaqzan, Salaman, and Absal. The first, living alone on an island, by the use of his reason alone attains to God and reaches full spiritual maturity. The other two, Salaman and Absal, living in the midst of their fellows, rediscover their faith, attaining their progress through the ways of religion.

The Qur'an, for its part, sums up these two approaches in a single person, Abraham, the example for believers. Describing the initial beginnings of awareness that enabled Abraham to rediscover God by a process of the elimination of false gods and idols, which had served as veils over his *fitra*, the Qur'an recounts:

[Remember the day when] Abraham said to his father Azar: "Do you take idols for gods? I see you, you and your people, have clearly gone astray." So we have shown to Abraham [Our] mighty dominion over the heaven and the earth, so that he should be anchored in certitude. When night encompassed him, he saw the star and said, "This is my Lord!" But when it had disappeared, he said: "I do not like those who disappear." When he saw the moon which rose in the sky, he said: "This is my Lord!" But when it had disappeared, he said: "If my Lord does not guide me, I shall be of those who go astray." When he saw the sun as it arose, he said: "This is my Lord, it is the greatest!" But when it had disappeared, he said: "O my people! I disown all that you associate with God. I turn my face, as a pure believer, toward Him who has created the heavens and the earth, and I am not among those who associate [anything with Him]." (*Al An'am* 6.74-79)

While he had come to God by the re-awakening of his *fitra*, by means of the use of his reason, Abraham represents also a way of religion, the *Hanifiyya*. The etymology of *Hanifiyya* suggests a "tending" toward religion or the right path, and the search for this path.[13] This quest is continuous, for no one can remain all their life on the right path but deviates from time to time, and then tries to recover the *fitra*, the way and the balance, so as to increase their faith and their closeness to God. Concerning this, the Qur'an says: "Submit yourself humbly to the Religion, as a pure believer (*hanif*), according to the *fitra* [original disposition] which God has given to human beings in creating them" (*Ar-Rum* 30.30).

In fact, it seems that some individuals have closely followed this Qur'anic injunction well before the message of Islam, for pre-Islamic Arabia knew – apart from Judaism and Christianity and their different communities – people who were known as *hunafa'* [*pl. of hanif*], followers of Abraham. These *hunafa'* were believing monotheists who did not have ritual observances or well-developed laws but who were characterized by their faith in a unique God and by trust in God. For this reason, the Qur'an calls them Muslims before the Qur'anic revelation was sent down, while the Qur'an awards to Abraham two titles, *hanif* and *muslim*, as if the two terms were interchangeable: "Abraham was neither a Jew nor a Christian, but he was a pure believer (*hanif*), submissive toward God (*muslim*), not one of those who associate [things or creatures with God]" (*Al Imran* 3.67). In a prayer that Abraham pronounced with his son Ishmael, he also said: "Our Lord! Make, from us two, believers who will be submissive to You; and make of our descendants a community which will submit to You (*ummatan muslimatan*); show us the rites that we should observe, and forgive us! You are, surely, the Ever Forgiving, the Most Merciful!" (*Al Baqara* 2.128).

The way of Abraham and the two Islams
The way of Abraham, also known as both *hanifiyya* and *islam,* corresponds to what we can name Islam in the wide sense, a faith in God and a constant return to the way of God and to the balance, which is distinct from Islam in the restricted sense, i.e., the religious identity of those who have believed in Muhammad and followed his message. In fact, the Qur'an uses the term *islam* and its adjective *muslim* according to two repertoires: one for those who have followed the Prophet Muhammad, and one when it speaks of the religion of Abraham: "Who therefore professes a religion more beautiful than the one who submits all of their self to God (*aslama*), doing good and following the religion of Abraham, a pure believer (*hanif*), whom God has taken for a friend?" (*An-Nisa'* 4.125).

This Islam in the wide sense, an Islam which pre-dates the Qur'anic revelation, will be like a matrix for all those religions acceptable to God. For this reason, the Qur'an says: "The religion for God is Islam"(*Al Imran* 3.19).[14] This verse has been explained by rigorists and some traditional scholars from the middle ages right up to our day as meaning that the only religion accepted by God is Islam in the narrow sense, to the exclusion of all other faiths. However, it is clear that an interpretation which has coherence with Qur'anic theology and terminology signifies rather islam in the wider sense, which infuses all revealed religions, of which it is the heart. For example, the following verse relativizes community affiliation or religious identity, putting the emphasis on the heart of faith in a unique God who never abandons humankind: "There are those [among the people of the Book] who say: 'Be Jews, or be Christians, and you will be rightly guided.' Reply to them: That which counts is the religion of Abraham, a pure believer (*hanif*), who was not one of those who associate [things or creatures with God] (*Al Baqara* 2.135).

Islam in the wider sense represents therefore the kernel of all spiritual and religious experience, individual or collective, through which human beings recognize the oneness of God and put their trust in God. It follows, on the one hand, that every personal religious and spiritual experience not identified with one or another of the religions is acceptable as a personal quest, according to the example of Abraham. On the other hand, the religions or ways which draw their inspiration from this *islam,* i.e., from this religion of Abraham, in other words the religions called Abrahamic, are considered according to the Qur'an as pure religions: "Religion which is pure is that which is devoted to God" (*Az-Zumar* 39.3).

One also finds in the Qur'an that Noah, Moses, the apostles of Christ, and all the prophets whose mission is part of the economy of the Reminder, as also their followers, call themselves Muslims, believers in God, who trust in him and give themselves to him.[15] However, we do not find here a claim on the part of Islam (in the narrower sense) over other religions, but an affirmation of belonging to the same economy of Reminder. For this reason, the religions founded by those prophets who call themselves Muslims in the Qur'an are also named by their own specific names, as for example Judaism and Christianity. It is as if the Qur'an has two repertoires, on the one hand a repertoire beyond identities of religious affiliations, which tends to show unity in diversity, and on the other hand a repertoire that names identities and shows the specific properties belonging to each. The Muslim religion also finds itself intrinsically linked to two trajectories of universality and particularity, the first when it comes to the most fundamental level of faith related to the innate predisposition (*fitra*), and the second related to the history of the Muslim community guided by the Qur'anic revelation.

3. Covenants and Revelations

Fadi Daou

"Covenant" is a fundamental concept in Jewish and Christian tradition that defines the relationship between God and human beings. Covenant is the arena where revelation is both made known and understood. In fact, covenant is the ground of the revelation of God and the transfiguration of humanity. If we separate revelation from covenant, the result is to split the human–divine relationship into two, between the categories of dogma (intellect) and ritual (religious practice), a division which lacks any historical or spiritual depth. In other words, to consider revelation apart from covenant is to turn God into an idol and to alienate human beings from their true vocation, for Christ has come to liberate humanity from all the seductions of religious display and empty observances. It is because people have sought to consider revelation in separation from the covenant of love and union between God and human beings that Christian theology has sometimes found itself in a cul de sac, where it is difficult to grasp the mystery of the universal history of salvation, and the place that other religions have to play in this mystery.

This chapter therefore attempts to present a Christian theology of the religious history of humankind in general and of Islam in particular, from the perspective of the covenant of love between God and humanity.

Covenant Theology and Revelation

The biblical structure of covenant

The Bible is the record of successive covenants made by God with humanity. The prophet Hosea explains to the people of Israel the meaning of the covenant God has made with them, a covenant which God will not cease to renew, despite their infidelity.

Hosea writes, in the name of the Lord:

> I will make for you a covenant on that day with the wild animals, the birds of the air, and the creeping things of the ground; and I will abolish the bow, the sword, and war from the land; and I will make you lie down in safety. And I will take you for my wife for ever; I will take you for my wife in righteousness and in justice, in steadfast love, and in mercy. I will take you for my wife in faithfulness; and you shall know the Lord. On that day I will answer, says the Lord, I will answer the heavens and they shall answer the earth; and the earth shall answer the grain, the wine, and the oil, and they shall answer Jezreel; and I will sow him for myself in the land. And I will have pity on Lo-ruhamah, and I will say to Lo-ammi, "You are my people"; and he shall say, "You are my God."[1] (Hosea 2:18-23)

This biblical text gives a cosmic dimension to this covenant, including along with human beings the whole of creation, represented by the beasts of the fields, the birds of the air, and the creeping things of the ground. We see from this that God's universal love embraces not only all humanity, but also all God's creatures.

This covenant is founded on a group of values defined by God, which constitute a kind of chart guiding the relationship between those betrothed. These values are righteousness, justice, steadfast love, mercy, and faithfulness. God promises to act with human beings according to these values, and he expects from human beings in return behaviour guided by this chart in their relationship to him as well as toward others.

Two clear results follow: peace among human beings, for war and its weapons will be broken; and heavenly blessings in response to the expectations of the earth. Furthermore, when human beings live their lives in harmony with this covenant and its demands, they enter into true knowledge of God. They recognize this Lordship over their life, and give him thanks through making offerings, signs both of the work of their hands and of God's blessing.

Hosea's account of the covenant is very striking and unusual when it comes to the relationship of God to the children who are the outcome of the prophet's engagement with prostitution. While by their symbolic names they seem to be excluded from all means of grace, God, through his steadfast love and mercy, not only includes them in his covenant but makes them the children of his choice. Lo-Ruhama, who was unloved, becomes the beloved of God. And Lo-Ammi, the excluded one, will be called by God "my people."

This biblical parable calls us to be particularly attentive to God's universal love and mercy and his relationship to human beings, and to be open to the subtleties of interpretation suggested by Hosea. Often, we are tempted to reduce the love of God and his generosity to the measure of our own self-centred calculations and interests. In such a debased logic, the covenant with God becomes similar to a business contract or to a dispute concerning rights of sale.

Covenant, the context of revelation

The relationship between God and humanity, which the Bible calls "covenant," cannot be understood as a form of contract. For "covenant" represents a commitment which cannot be undone, a commitment of love and goodwill by God toward human beings. History becomes the place for this saving love to be made known, a love which expresses itself in the words and divine actions which together constitute revelation, as well as being the means of God's active and illuminating presence in our midst. In this way, revelation can be seen as a process of human education in which the faithful, both individually and corporately, are enabled to grow in their love for God and in their understanding of the divine mystery. In other words, covenant is the binding relationship God makes with humanity, and revelation is the record of this relationship. Thus we see in the Bible that the love of God and the knowledge of God are inseparable. By accepting divine love, and by living our lives in the love of God and of our neighbour, we are drawn into a deeper knowledge and experience of God: this is our unique pathway to spiritual growth. The covenant, when understood in this way, provides the basis and the completion of the relationship of God with humanity and is the key by which we interpret revelation.

Furthermore, God's ultimate will for human beings, according to Christian theology, is to share with us his own divine nature, rather than to teach us a list of truths. In this way, divine revelation becomes for believers the source of life and of union with God, rather than a code to follow in order for us to "succeed" in our lives in the kind of way that we might pass a final examination. "By this revelation," teaches the Second Vatican Council, "the invisible God (see Col. 1:15, 1 Tim. 1:17) from the fullness of his love addresses men and women as his friends (see Ex. 33:11; John 15:14-15) and lives among them (see Bar. 3:38), in order to invite and receive them into his own company" (*Dei Verbum* 2).

The successive covenants are therefore like grafts into the tree of divine–human relationship, while the revelations represent branches of the tree which display its character and bear fruits of grace and holiness.

The Universal Covenant of God with Humanity

The covenant with Adam

From its beginning, human history has been marked by the closeness of the relationship between God and human beings. In fact, the likeness of men and women to God (cf. Gen. 1:26) represents a very special way in which God is linked with his human creation. According to the biblical perspective, to be in the image and according to the likeness of God indicates a kind of kinship (see Gen. 5.3) and a sharing of responsibility.

Having breathed into their nostrils the breath of life (cf. Gen. 2:7), God blesses man and woman, and entrusts to them the care of all creation (cf. Gen. 1:28-31; 2:15). The psalmist celebrates in song this confidence and trust which God has placed in humanity: "Lord,... what are human beings that you are mindful of them, mortals that you care for them? Yet you have made them a little lower than God, and crowned them with glory and honour. You have given them dominion over the works of your hands" (Ps. 8:4-6).

The first state of creation shows this natural relationship between God and human beings, represented by their living together in the garden of Eden. It is a plan for mutual communion which God established between himself and humanity (cf. Gen. 2:8). This is the first covenant, which expresses the commitment of God's love toward human beings and the great trust that he places in them. At the same time, the covenant obliges human beings to face up to their responsibilities, since they are appointed by God to be the guardians of creation.

Then the Bible tells us how, from the very beginning, human beings failed to honour their responsibility and disobeyed God. Through self-centredness and foolishness they transgressed the order of nature by eating of the tree of the knowledge of good and evil (cf. Gen. 3:1-7), and, through jealousy, man has offended against the sacredness of life by killing his brother (cf. Gen. 4:1-16). In fact, through refusing to take up his role as "steward," man broke the covenant with God and brought disorder into the creation. So when the Lord asks him to account for his responsibilities with the question, "Where is your brother?" through the voice of Cain he replies, "I do not know; am I my brother's keeper?" (Gen. 4:9).

The renewal of the covenant with Noah

When human beings betrayed the trust that God had placed in them and broke the covenant, God did not abandon them. Despite these beginnings, the history of God with human beings will be founded upon divine mercy, which is the bearer of hope and new life for humanity.

And so, despite Adam and Eve's disobedience, God did not withdraw the trust he had placed in them. Man would continue to be steward and hold responsibility for creation, and God promised him victory over the force of evil which pursued him (cf. Gen. 2:14-15). Then when God saw that the wickedness of humanity was spreading itself over the earth, he repented from having created humankind. He wished to wipe out human beings from the face of the earth, yet he remembered Noah, who had found grace in his eyes (cf. Gen. 6:1-21). God therefore spared him from the flood, along with two of each living creature. And he renewed his covenant with Noah when they went out from the ark: "As for me, I am establishing my covenant with you and your descendants after you, and with every living creature that is with you" (Gen. 9:9-10).

The first covenant with Adam, renewed with Noah, is "archetypal" rather than historical. It teaches us that God, through his mercy, is always greater than the sinful heart of humanity. And it also shows that this covenant is universal and includes the whole of humankind, from first beginnings up to our own days, and to the end of time.

So we see that this regenerative mercy does not just act to recreate humanity, as if each time the accounts were set at zero and a new story of the divine–human relationship begins. For there is really only one salvation history with many covenants. From one covenant to the next, God takes forward a patient and progressive strategy of education with human beings, opening their hearts both to the knowledge of his person and his will.

The Covenant with Abraham

Abraham, a blessing for the nations

Subsequent to the universal covenant, made first with Adam and then with Noah, the Bible presents us with another form of covenant that brings about the distinctive historic and religious identity of three traditions: Jewish, Christian, and Muslim. This is the covenant concluded with Abraham. This covenant has its own particular place in history, while at the same time playing a formative role in religious development.

God declared to Abraham: "I am God Almighty; walk before me, and be blameless. And I will make my covenant between me and you, and will make you exceedingly numerous" (Gen. 17:1-2). Two promises are linked to this covenant: a posterity which will make Abraham "the ancestor of a multitude of nations" (cf. Gen. 17:5), and a land to be given as an inheritance to him and to his descendants (cf. Gen. 15:18; 17:8). Furthermore, this covenant will be sealed by a sign in the flesh of Abraham himself and of his people, the sign of circumcision (cf. Gen.17:11).

This covenant with its particularity does not replace the universal dimension of the relationship between God and humanity, but opens a new path within this relationship. Despite the particular nature of this covenant, with its promises and special signs, we must not forget the origin of Abraham's vocation, when God willed to make him a blessing for all the families of the earth. The Lord says to him, "I will make of you a great nation, and I will bless you, and make your name great, so that you will be a blessing ... and in you all the families of the earth shall be blessed (Gen. 12:2-3).

And so this new form of covenant confers on Abraham a particular place in God's plan. No longer is it God alone who engages with human beings and their salvation. He invites human beings to collaborate in fulfilling his divine plan, in the carrying of his blessing to all the nations on earth. Within the covenant, human beings are from now on responsible not for their own lives alone, but for those of others. The universal dimension of Abraham's mission is revealed when he intercedes on behalf of the town of Sodom, seeking to spare it from the judgement appointed because its people have turned aside from God's commandments (cf. Gen. 18:16-33).

Each life on earth is called to be a life which is blessed, and Abraham becomes, like all believers who follow after him in this covenant, the instrument of divine blessing. Each believer following the path of Abraham is a kind of "priest of God," who by keeping faith with the covenant conveys divine blessing to others. The divine plan for the salvation and sanctification of the world has already been put into action. With Abraham we see a change of strategy. It is by means of human intermediaries that God wishes to sanctify the whole of humanity from within, just as leaven acts upon dough. The covenant with Abraham introduces us to the mystery of divine patience.

The blessing of Abraham by Melchizedek

This special role and great responsibility carry with them the risk of leading the people of the covenant toward an attitude of superiority toward others, or perhaps even to their exclusion. The encounter between Abraham and Melchizedek finds its meaning in confronting this temptation to exclusivity (Gen. 14:17-24). In fact, within the story of this encounter there is an exchange of roles which is highly significant. Melchizedek, who represents the alien or the other, is not party to the covenant concluded between God and Abraham. And yet he becomes for Abraham the instrument or means of grace. The text makes it clear that it is Melchizedek who pronounces a blessing for Abraham with the presentation of bread and wine as an offering, while Abraham shows his recognition of Melchizedek's sacerdotal role by pledging to him a tithe from all that belongs to him.

Different interpretations of this passage have been put forward, and it retains a certain enigmatic character. For myself, I draw from this story the following lesson: the covenant concluded by God with a person or a people is surpassed by the experience of God's actions in the world and of the depth and extraordinary resonance of salvation history, which is without limit. It is as if God wished Abraham to understand that his vocation to bless the earth and his role of universal intercessor in no way limits the freedom of God in his relations with humanity. Therefore, the Abrahamic covenant does not exclude other forms of showing divine grace to the world.

St Irenaeus affirms that "there is only the one and the same God, who, from the beginning to the end, by various means [economies] comes to the aid of the human race."[2] And so the universal covenant made with Adam and Noah retains its value and effect right across the varied religious experiences of humanity. The Abrahamic covenant does not replace it, neither does it oppose it or claim the same identity. Rather, it is like a catalyst that has been inserted within it. It would be wrong, therefore, to deprive the first covenant of all divine grace, by seeing it as simply the reflection of human efforts in the quest to make sense of life and to reach out to the absolute.

In his book *Les Saints 'paiens' dans l'Ancien Testament* (The 'pagan' saints in the Old Testament), Jean Daniélou stated that "the cosmic covenant is already a supernatural covenant. It is not of a different order to the Mosaic covenant or the covenant in Christ."[3] And Jacques Dupuis suggests that the religious traditions of humanity bear witness to the covenant with Noah, and represent an intervention by God in the history of the nations which is both personal and universal in character.[4]

We can therefore conclude from the example of Melchizedek that the covenant with Adam and Noah represents a permanent station from which we may view the various manifestations of God and his actions, actions which are adapted to the circumstances both of persons and of nations. Seen from this perspective, the whole of humanity is "people of God," and the one and only God is God of all peoples. This means that "all people, all nations, all cultures and all civilizations have their own role to fulfil and a special place in the mysterious plan of God and in the universal history of salvation."[5]

The evolution of the biblical concept of revelation

In the Abrahamic covenant, God reveals himself in his closeness to human beings, who walk in his presence and in his sight, which is both protective and benevolent. The Bible describes for us how God takes care both of Hagar and Ishmael, and of Abraham and Isaac. So when Hagar ran away from her mistress Sarah who mistreated her, the angel of the Lord came to console her by announcing the birth of Ishmael, whose descendants will be multiplied by God. Hagar interprets this divine intervention in these words: "You are God who sees me" (Gen. 16:13).

It is remarkable that at the moment of the testing of Abraham, called by God to offer his son Isaac as a sacrifice, we find the same expression is used in order to convey this infinite confidence in God. In response to Isaac's demand to know where is the lamb for the burnt offering, Abraham replies: "God will be sure to see the lamb for the sacrifice, my son" (Gen. 22:8). Thus, after God commands Abraham to spare his son and sacrifice a ram in his place, Abraham names the place of the sacrifice "God sees" (Gen. 22:14).

It is certainly true that when the covenant was made with Noah, this theme of divine providence was introduced (cf. Gen. 7:1), without however being at this point the revelation of a fundamental truth describing God's relationship with humanity. We find the deeper sense of this reality of divine providence expressed by King Abimelech, when he says: "God is with you in all that you do" (Gen. 21:22). Thus it seems that with the Abrahamic covenant a new dimension of revelation makes an appearance, where human beings become conscious of the presence of God in the events of their lives. This happens as if the separation caused by the sin of Adam and Eve, which caused them to be expelled from the Garden of Eden, the place of the Lord's presence, is overcome by God's entry into "the garden of humanity" where human life and history is played out. Since then, God "sees" human beings, engages with them (cf. Gen. 18:33) and shares in the writing of their sacred history. We should note that this revelation does not inscribe itself into a text, nor does it leave literary evidences. The world itself becomes its literature, and life becomes its ink.

The revelation to Moses and the renewal of the Abrahamic covenant

From a theological perspective, the Abrahamic covenant enters a new phase with the revelation to Moses, which in turn acknowledges its inheritance. The Old Testament witnesses many renewals of the Abrahamic covenant. After Moses, there will be the renewal of the covenant and of the promise with David (cf. 2 Sam. 7:5-16). With each renewal, a new dimension of the covenant appears, as with the Torah with Moses, and the kingship with David. But the prophets, for their part, call for an "interiorization" of the covenant, as a reminder that it consists essentially in the personal relationship with God rather than in expectation of an outwardly visible fulfilment of the promises.

Thus Jeremiah proclaims:

> The days are surely coming, says the Lord, when I will make a new covenant with the house of Israel and the house of Judah. It will not be like the covenant that I made with their ancestors when I took them by the hand to bring them out of the land of Egypt—a covenant that they broke, though I was their husband, says the Lord. But this is the covenant that I will make with the house of Israel after those days, says the Lord: I will put my law within them, and I will write it on their hearts; and I will be their God, and they shall be my people. (Jer. 31:31-33)

Moses and the gift of the Torah

The renewal of the covenant with Moses constitutes the founding event of Judaism. It is also the source of a new revelation, chiefly expressed in God's liberation of the Hebrew people from the yoke of Pharaoh and by the giving of the Torah. The biblical passages which record this event insist on continuity with the Abrahamic alliance, while revealing its particular dimension, the founding of the Hebrew people and of their religion. So, when the bible recounts the sending of Moses by God to free his people from slavery in Egypt, the biblical record is clear both on the continuity of the covenant and the newness of the revelation. God says "I have also heard the groaning of the Israelites whom the Egyptians are holding as slaves, and I have remembered my covenant." And the Lord promises, "I will bring you into the land that I swore to give to Abraham, Isaac, and Jacob" (Ex. 6:8). But in contrast, God makes Moses understand that with this renewal of the covenant, he reveals himself differently: "I appeared to Abraham, Isaac, and Jacob as God Almighty, but by my name 'The Lord' I did not make myself known to them" (Ex. 6:3).

After the exodus from Egypt and the renewal of the covenant in the desert of Sinai, God gave the Jewish people a new revelation, which brought about a new form of relationship between God and his people. In addition to Abraham's trust in God, the believer will now be required to know his word and to put it into practice. The Torah becomes so important that it takes first place in the Jewish understanding of covenant, for it is the powerful sign of the presence of God with his people. The term "covenant" meant, from now on, not only the relationship which unites believers to God, but also the tablets of the Law, enclosed in the ark (cf. 1 Kings 8:21). The Torah became in reality the "code of the covenant," under the form of the Decalogue and its development (Ex. 20:1-17; 20:22-23, 33).

Then, when Moses passed on to the people all the words and rules revealed by the Lord, "all the people answered with one voice, and said, 'All the words that the Lord has spoken we will do'" (Ex. 24:3). The revelation is to be inscribed in "the book of the covenant" (Ex. 24:7). As the people are sprinkled with the blood of sacrifices, Moses declares: "See the blood of the covenant that the Lord has made with you in accordance with all these words" (Ex. 24:8).

The renewal of the Abrahamic covenant with Moses is accompanied by a new revelation, that of the Torah, and gives birth to the Jewish religion. To return to the image of the tree representing the relationship of God with humanity, with Moses we are still here in the Abrahamic graft, but with a new branch stretching out to bring forth fruits of grace in the Jewish religion and its history.

The Permanence of the Covenants

As he proclaims Christ the Messiah of Israel and universal Saviour, the apostle Paul tackles the difficult question of the significance of the refusal to accept this new covenant by many of the Jewish people. Chapters 9 to 11 of his letter to the Romans set forth his reflection concerning the destiny of the Jewish branch of the covenant following the coming of Christ. Confronting this problem, Paul states categorically, "The gifts and the judgement of God are irrevocable." (Rom. 11:29). Jacques Dupuis sums up Paul's response in these terms: "Israel was – and continued to be – the people of God; the covenant with Moses endured without a break, thanks to the love and faithfulness of God."[6]

We have to recognize, however, that not all the New Testament writings treat this thorny question in the same way. The Letter to the Hebrews, for example, presents a contrast to Pauline thought. It insists on the fact that the old covenants and promises are all fulfilled in Christ. From then onward, it is the glorified Christ, our great high priest, who assures human beings of access to God. However, if the author of this epistle insists so forcibly on the fulfilment and displacement of the old covenant by the new, he is equally committed to showing the continuity between the two Testaments.

In fact, fulfilment does not mean a replacement of the false by the true, but a confirmation of the image of the unchangeable heavenly reality prefigured in the Old Testament (cf. Heb. 8:5; 9:24). The fullness of the revelation in Jesus Christ can only be understood in the light of the actual time of fulfilment, not by following a chronological outline of history. That is why the Epistle to the Hebrews begins by affirming the concurrence of renewal of the covenant in Jesus Christ and the arrival of the "last times" (Heb. 1:1-2). What is more, for Christians the Old Testament, being part of the Bible, is read and prayed over in the light of Christ, without ceasing to be in itself the living word of God for those of Jewish faith.

With the Second Vatican Council, the Catholic Church has been liberated from a theology of substitution in which Israel had been replaced by the church, rendering the Mosaic covenant void. The Council recognized implicitly the permanence of the covenant in the Jewish religion (cf. *Lumen genitum* 16, *Nostra aetate: Declaration of Vatican II on the Relations of the Church with Non-Christian Religions*, 4). The Christian position, according to Jacques Dupuis, is that of a covenant with two independent paths within the same organic plan of salvation. "For the Christian faith, the Christ Event could not exist without Israel, nor through Israel as an abstract or ideal concept; on the other hand Israel would never have been chosen by God except as the people from whom would come Jesus of Nazareth."[7]

It is of crucial important that the church should recognize the permanence of the Jewish revelation, not only for relations with Judaism, but for Christian theology of religious pluralism as well. We have therefore been able to leave behind a linear and chronological scheme of the history of salvation, where that which comes after annuls that which comes before. However, the concurrent existence of two revelations, Jewish and Christian, must necessarily direct theology toward new avenues of research. The need to uphold the unity of the divine plan of salvation and the universality of Christ, unique mediator between God and humanity, does not necessarily lead us to a reading of the Jewish revelation solely in terms of the Christ Event. The form of interdependence between the two revelations which Dupuis puts forward does not convince me. For we must be able to infer the place of Israel in the divine plan beginning from the Torah itself, written into the Abrahamic covenant, and not only according to the messianic perspective fulfilled in Jesus Christ.

Recognizing the permanence of the Jewish revelation should lead us to understand and appreciate it from the viewpoint of the people who live it out in their lives. Even though the Messianic expectation is undeniably present in their tradition, for the Jews the Torah represents the greatest gift that God has given to them, and to humanity. That Christ has come to fulfil and not to abolish the Law and the prophets (cf. Matt. 5:17) encourages to see this permanence of the Jewish revelation as a source of grace and a form of the covenant of love between God and the children of this covenant. It is not a question, therefore, of a linear approach, where what follows replaces that which comes before, nor of parallel ways that have no link between them. The Jewish and Christian revelations are rather two branches of the same tree, growing from the same Abrahamic graft. The question which remains is whether this particular status of Judaism from the Christian point of view is unique, or is perhaps relevant for Christian interpretation of other religious traditions and their link with the covenant.

The Muslim religion and the Abrahamic covenant

In the *Dogmatic Constitution on the Church*, Vatican II recognized that Muslims as well Christians worship the one God and affirmed that they profess the faith of Abraham (cf. *Lumen gentium* 16). I believe we are still far from having exhausted all the theological richness of such a declaration. Since the time of Abraham, humanity has been called to recognize that God is one, and that there are no others. God is the God of all. Thus, all who recognize themselves as being of the Abrahamic faith – in the first instance the Jews, the Christians and the Muslims – must be the witnesses of this truth and its guardians from all forms of "associationism," whether theoretical or practical.

The Council's affirmation not only closes the door on those who still today maintain that Christians and Muslims do not worship the same God, but regards believers of both communities as participants in one act of faith, different in form, but unique both in its foundation and in its conclusiveness. In their Pastoral Letter on Muslim–Christian relations, entitled "Together before God," the Oriental Catholic patriarchs teach that "the co-existence between Christians and Muslims is not a parallel co-existence. . . on the contrary it includes an intimate encounter in faith in the one God, in the hope which relies on his effective grace and in the love of God for others."[8] Speaking of faith in the Oneness of God, Christian de Chergé affirms, for his part, that "if God is truly unique, the God of Islam and the God of Jesus Christ cannot be a plurality."[9]

Islam in the Abrahamic covenant

There is more in common between Christianity and Islam than a monotheistic faith. The Council was able gladly to affirm that the monotheistic faith of Muslims belongs – as the Qur'an strongly testifies – to the covenant with Abraham. This shows that Muslims truly belong within the very select company of the faithful who are children of Abraham. The Qur'an clearly issues an invitation to an Abrahamic faith in the one God to whom human beings should submit and live out their lives in his merciful sight. It is even true to say that the Qur'anic message, at its heart, belongs to Abrahamic faith even more than do Judaism and Christianity. In other words, of the three monotheistic faiths, Islam is today the most Abrahamic.

The reason we can say this is because the Jewish and Christian religions both identify themselves as belonging to a covenant which includes further revelations, bringing developments to the faith of Abraham. Whereas, with Islam, its theological message remains very close to the Abrahamic faith, for it is intended as a reminder and an invitation to rediscover this faith in its original form, named "hanifism." And so, for Islam, Abraham represents the supreme example for believers, whereas for Jews and Christians he is their father in faith.

What is the theological significance of this Islamic–Christian relationship within the Abrahamic covenant? And what is the link between the Muslim religion and the origins of the biblical revelation? Taking the example of the Mosaic revelation, is Islam a renewal of the Abrahamic covenant rather than a new revelation: the Qur'anic revelation? To put it metaphorically, was there a new graft upon the Abrahamic branch of the tree of salvation, which sprang forth in the seventh century after Jesus Christ? To put the question in a more traditional form, what is the place of Islam in God's plan, from the Christian point of view?

Christian de Chergé adopts a threefold approach toward this question. Thus he expresses his deep desire to be united with the Father, so as to be able to see his brother and sister Muslims with God's vision, and so to discover "from on high" and with joy the theological dimension in their religion and their life. Then he allows himself to live with these questions, even without any replies. Thus he says, "I am learning in order to discover better the identities and even the complicities of today, including those of faith, not to fix on the other the idea of faith that I form for myself, which my Church perhaps has transmitted to me, nor even what the Church may actually be able to say about it from a majority viewpoint."[10] Then, when the desire for theological truth and for the development of relations of solidarity between Christians and Muslims overtakes this spiritual patience, he launches himself into the adventure of a search for answers, even provisional ones. "A pathway which is already ancient in Muslim lands has taught me," he says, "that actually you cannot live as a person who prays among others who pray without reaching out, with some impatience, toward the divine meaning of that which, humanly speaking, separates us."[11]

We can observe that it is often when one is led into a context which provides an experience of solidarity and of dialogue that this work of theological research produces its best results. Furthermore, research in this area does not only have the benefit of bringing clarity to interreligious relationships; it also becomes a source for the renewal and development of Christian theology.

The decree on the missionary activity of the church (Vatican II) invites the local churches, each in its own sociocultural context, to develop a renewed process of theological reflection which takes account of the wisdom and customs of the peoples who are found in its territory (*Ad gentes: Decree of Vatican Council II on the Missionary Activity of the Church* 22). In harmony with this appeal to a theology which is both contextual and intercultural, I have chosen to present in what follows two approaches to Islam and its place in the divine plan, starting from the work – with divergent results – of two Lebanese theologians: Michel Hayek and Youakim Moubarac.

Hayek and the mystery of Ishmael

In his quest for a Christian theology of Islam, Michel Hayek assigns the Qur'anic religion to pre-biblical religious history. For him, if Islam can be understood as a form of Abrahamic religion, it is according to an Abrahamic *hanafitism*, "which is above all a form of the religion of Adam, a primordial religion, the unchangeable religion of innate human identity (*fitra*)."[12] Hayek links Islam theologically with Ishmael rather than with Abraham. Thus Ishmael represents the first phase of the life of Abraham before the promises, when his name was still Abram (cf. Gen. 17:5). Islam remains in this sense at the level of biblical history, but does not enter into sacred history. It represents rather the global and original religion of monotheism, and belongs to the universal Adam–Noah covenant and not to the Abrahamic covenant. "As descending from Ishmael, Islam has recovered the archaic traditions which Abram had bequeathed to his elder son, so halting religious evolution at Hammurabi."[13] Islam is like "An Old Testament to the Old Testament."[14]

For Hayek, this approach to Islam does not represent a negative conception of a religion overtaken by time and history. Rather, it is a matter of a particular conception of the religious history of humanity. Thus the fulfilment by Islam of the promise made to Abraham cannot be placed in the context of historical development, but rather in a return to the origins of time. The religion therefore resembles a white pearl, which Muhammad has received the mission to cleanse from the deposits of time. While the Christian tradition considers that, from Abraham to Jesus, time grew and fulfilled its goal according to a divine tutorship that leads humanity progressively toward an encounter that is its complete fulfilment, Hayek considers that symbolically "the Qur'an can be nothing other than the archaeological discovery of a manuscript in a family property."[15] Making bold use of metaphor, Hayek compares the Qur'an to "a kernel hard to crack," by comparison to the gospel, which is represented by a "grain of mustard" that grows slowly throughout history.

This approach is founded on a particular theological reading of Islam that places it outside the scheme of the covenant. For Hayek,

the promise of which the Qur'an speaks is rather a "testament," a "legacy" (*'ahd,wasiya;* cf. *Al-Baqara* 2.124.132) which does not add up to any "covenant" in the biblical sense of the word; for in concluding a pact with human beings from their origins, and in renewing this pact with each of the prophets, God does not engage himself; he "receives the pact" (*akhdh al-Mithaq*; cf. 3.81.187), the given word by which human beings commit themselves to faithfulness.[16]

The Muslim religion is here represented as "a desert religion," one of adoration *par excellence*, but not of love or of "familiarity" with God. This leads Hayek to say that "to believe in the God of Abraham for Islam, is to entrust oneself to his will, without the concept of relating to the One who is both Love and Hope."[17]

However, despite his trenchant view of Islam, placing it outside the history of the Jewish and Christian covenants and revelations, Hayek does not hesitate, though not without caution, to recognize an inspiration and a divine grace in the work of Muhammad. "In the measure where Muhammad has responded sincerely to that grace and in the measure where the Qur'an carries the trace of the truth which he held, it is in this measure, conditional and limited certainly, but real, that Muhammad and the Qur'an can be called 'inspired.'"[18] In this sense, Muhammad can be considered as an extra-biblical prophet. For this, Hayek finds support in St Ephraem, who saw that, in the source of water springing up in favour of Ishmael (cf. Gen. 21:19),[19] representing the Spirit of God, all the children of Hagar have already received a baptism, "the baptism of tears," so dear to the Syriac tradition.[20]

Recognized as an inspired religion, Islam may also have a providential function in the plan of God. Faced with his brother Isaac, jealous and exclusive, who kept for himself and his descendants the treasure of the paternal blessing, Ishmael proclaims the global election of believing humanity which issues from Adam, and holds to this position until his brother grants him, having first of all claimed them, the universal provisions of God.

Hayek also considers that the negations in the Qur'an of Christian truths remain conditional, waiting upon Christians to prove the contrary. Islam becomes a kind of "judgment upon a Church which is divided and failing, and it will continue to be so until the Church becomes what it should always be, the Church of the Beatitudes."[21] Meanwhile, he focuses this hope on the expectation of the return of Christ, and the universal messianic reconciliation which will then be brought about by Christ, the Messiah of Israel and "Caliph of the eschatological times."

Moubarac and "biblical Islam"

For Youakim Moubarac, faithful disciple of Louis Massignon, Islam is fundamentally Abrahamic and is part of the biblical covenant. His thesis on Abraham in the Qur'an[22] arrived at conclusions quite distant if not opposed to the theology of Islam presented by Hayek. Moubarac is convinced of the centrality of Abraham in Islam, and believes that by considering just the person of Abraham, we come to engage with practically the whole religious conception of the Qur'an. He states that "the name Abraham is not simply and ingeniously added to the Qur'anic presentation. It marks an authentic appropriation, and reveals in the Qur'an a genuine return to the source of a doctrine, or rather the interior adoption within the Qur'an of a primitive religious attitude"[23] From this he reaches the definite conclusion that the faith of Abraham is the faith of Islam. Moreover, if Muslims share the monotheistic faith of Abraham, they also recognize themselves as included in the biblical dynamic of salvation through Ishmael. Moubarac regards the person of Ishmael in the Qur'an as

> reclaiming, despite the Jews, the biblical blessing given by the patriarch to his son who was chased into the desert. But this privilege accorded to the Arabs is not in order to separate them, rather it integrates them into a wider community, that of the believers in the

God of Abraham. We can even say that Ishmael, "biblical" prophet, draws them together with the people of the scriptures rather than separating them. However he also keeps them independent, with the whole of the Muslim world. For this biblical character is corroborated by that of *ummi,* separate and "without scripture."

And Moubarac concludes his description: "A 'biblical' people without scripture until the Qur'an"[24]

When Moubarac includes Islam in the Abrahamic covenant he does not, however, put Islam in the position of having a "derived legitimacy." On the contrary, through the place taken by Ishmael it recovers its status of autonomy and originality, even its mission toward the two other Abrahamic religions. In fact Moubarac, in accord with Hayek, presents Islam as a negative or "desert Abrahamism," represented appropriately by the figure of Ishmael. "The destiny of Ishmael" he says "is in some way essential to the promise given to Isaac, in order to prevent him from declining into racial exclusivism."[25] And further, for the benefit of Christians, this same desert Abrahamism may be seen to be linked to a Marian destiny, reminding us that "only faith is the deliverer of fecundity, and the bearer of fulfilment."[26] While for Claude Geffré, Islam constitutes a warning for the Christian theological conscience, in the sense that "it challenges it not to neglect the Jewish aspect of primitive Christianity, and to be critical of certain loose ways of speaking about the divinity of Jesus, which risk compromizing the absolute transcendence of God."[27]

The Islamic Revelation

In order to go further in exploring the Abrahamic graft on the tree of salvation, and the religions which belong to it, we have to recognize that the promises are derived from the covenant, and therefore secondary to it; the ultimate fulfilment of the covenant awaits the spreading abroad of God's blessings upon all of his creatures. In this sense, I note that even if Ishmael – according to the Jewish-Christian tradition

– is not the son of the promise, he remains nevertheless a son of the covenant and bearer of the divine blessing (cf. Gen.17,18-20;22.18).

Thanks to this distinction between the covenant and the promises, and giving the covenant priority in the divine plan, I follow Moubarac rather than Hayek regarding their theologies of Islam. Islam surely represents a specific branch on the tree of salvation, which springs forth from the Abrahamic graft, in common with Judaism and Christianity. As regards the irreducible identity of Israel, Claude Geffré asserts that there is also "an irreducible identity to the 'Ishmaelism' of Islam"[28]

But Islam, which confirms and represents the religion of Abraham, is not simply a pure reflection of the Abrahamic covenant. It also brings to this covenant its own proper content, which we find principally in the Qur'an and the Sunna, as well as in the various internal traditions of Islam such as in Shi'ism and the other Islamic confessions. Is it possible to go deeper, and form a view on the revelation of the Qur'an and on Muhammad's prophetic mission? Further, can a religion be recognized as belonging to the Abrahamic covenant simply because it claims to belong to it? Or does this link necessarily imply a divine revelation which makes educational and historical sense within this covenant? However to recognize the Qur'anic revelation and the prophethood of Muhammad brings us face to face with the dilemma of certain contradictions – at least in appearance and in the historic consciousness of the two religions – between this message and the status of Jesus Christ, Son of God and the fullness of revelation.

Obstacles in the way of recognition

Before examining these questions further, we need to be precise about one issue. Christians are often pressed by their Muslim partners in dialogue to give clear responses to these kinds of questions. Now it seems to me that to demand a categorical response to these questions sometimes hides an attitude, not of dialogue or of solidarity, but of unconscious rivalry, for which there are both structural and historic reasons. Islam, as much as Christianity, possesses a definitive character and a universal claim. These two religions are sometimes among the most insensitive so far as religious absolutism is concerned, as well as imperialism. If one does not keep a space between God, as absolute truth, and each of the religions claiming to be recipients of his revelation, one falls into a pernicious form of self-assertive group identity and spiritual pride, which transforms religion from a path of sanctity into a form of segregation and a force for coercion in the hands of the most powerful.

Furthermore, often the demand for recognition comes on the part of "religious authorities," those representing Christians or Muslims, and so there is a hidden motive. I am afraid that games of power hold the advantage over wishes for rapprochement in certain inter-religious quarters. Dialogue can sometimes become an instrument for the legitimation of authority or a claim on the part of a representative of one of the communities. No one bothers to ask, for example, if we can recognize or not the work of God in the life of persons such as Mother Teresa, Ghandi, or Badshah Khan. The work of the Spirit of God is recognizable in itself.

A certain vigilance is therefore necessary in order to discern between the work of God in human lives and religions and the dynamics of power, whether religious or clerical, which may not be purely at the service of this work. In the context of Islamic-Christian relations, we must not forget that history is strongly marked by this ideological manipulation of the two religions to the benefit of projects of domination. The collective memory of believers in the two religions is strongly marked by this historical face-to-face, and this tension between civilizations.

From this perspective, to demand a simple recognition, which does not take into account the history of interreligious relationships and the different approach of each of the two religions with its own limits when faced with the mystery of God and his covenant with humanity, will reflect a complex of inferiority or superiority which will drive one religion to seek a confirmation of its own religious identity as against the other. René Habachi, when he speaks of relations between the West and the Orient, does not hesitate to describe their attitudes toward each other as a reciprocal malady. "A superiority complex face to face with an inferiority complex – how can dialogue be possible? Dialogue between two deranged persons! Each in his own way shows his inability to understand the other, simply because he does not understand himself."[29] Furthermore, this attitude reflects an exclusivism, unconscious though it may be, which refuses to accept the integrity of each of the branches of the Abrahamic covenant and wishes to identify itself with the whole tree, even if that means cutting off all its branches.

What to do therefore? Some are inclined to take up the Qur'anic suggestions to leave it to God to come and help us – when we shall be in the beatific vision- to see more clearly into the differences and different theologies, and to turn for now toward mutual emulation in faithfulness to God and in service of the good (cf. *Al-Ma'ida* 5.48). For my part, I hope that instead of burdening our prophets and their divine messages with our sins of pride and the historical strife which followed them, we might concentrate on that religious authenticity and spiritual solidarity in which we are already united. Then we will be able to take a more lucid view and estimation of our differences. "Among simple people of good faith," writes Christian de Chergé, "these differences take a more familiar form; they have become integrated with the mutual contacts of day to day living. They show a friendly face which has traces of the divine. These very differences inspire respect for the ways of God and the human heart. And they are able to take their place in the calmness of prayer, and even, here or there, in prayer together."[30]

Sincere understanding of one another is therefore only possible in a climate of fellowship and spiritual solidarity, where believers from either side place themselves in complete humility before the mystery of God and his merciful love which excludes no one. With such an attitude, believers who seek a meaning to their differences travel together toward clarity, accepting the distinctiveness of the other, and deepening their interpretation of their own tradition. It is in such an Abrahamic spirit of mutual acceptance that, for example, the members of GRIC (Groupe de recherche islamo-chrétien), in their work *Ces Écritures qui nous questionnent* ['these scriptures which question us'] reach a concept more nuanced than that of "falsification," and arrive together at the following conviction: "We consider that the Muslim theory of *Tahrif* may today be perfectly addressed by the textual criticism of the Bible undertaken by Christians."[31]

Recognition of Islam

I believe that Christianity, without any compromise regarding its theological foundations, is able to recognize a revelation in the Qur'an and a prophetic dimension in the message of Muhammad. This recognition is derived from the Christian understanding of the history of salvation. In other words, Christians can only interpret the place of Islam in the history of salvation in the light of the mystery of Jesus Christ, universal saviour and the fullness of the revelation of God for humankind. To go further toward achieving clarity in this question, I believe that the key to interpretation is found in the divergence in the conception of time between Christianity and Islam. Hayek perceived this, except that he was mistaken in his choice of the different time zones. Islam is not in "archaic time," pre-biblical as he considers; it belongs to the Abrahamic covenant and therefore to biblical time. But it is Christ who, while taking part in biblical history, inaugurates another field of time, that of the *pleroma* or the fullness of time. And the mystery of Christ, eternal Word of God, incarnate, dead and risen for the salvation of all humanity, only discloses its meaning when it is addressed within its own field of time. When one affirms that Christ is the fullness of revelation and the completion of the divine plan, this should not be understood in terms of time which can be measured and evaluated as in chronology, but in terms of the eschatological dimension which has its own quality.

In consequence, the fact that Islam appeared in history after Christianity does not change the relationship of Christ to this religion, for this relationship is eschatological and not chronological. And that there has been a revelation after Christianity does not put in question the fullness of the revelation in Jesus Christ. In the light of these remarks, it does not contradict Christian faith to recognize a prophetic mission given to Muhammad, the messenger of Islam, not far removed from the mission of the biblical prophets of the Old Testament. In comparing the Qur'an to the Old Testament, R.C. Zaehner observed that "It is impossible to read these two books together without concluding that it is the same God who speaks in both: the prophetic accents cannot be doubted."[32] In fact Muhammad himself understood that God had commanded him to exhort his people to faithfulness to the Abrahamic covenant. As a "spokesperson" of God, Muhammad, from a Christian point of view is therefore a prophet of the Abrahamic covenant.

Covenants and revelations

Can Muhammad's message, written in the Qur'an, be a revelation? Certainly, for the Christian, the Qur'an cannot be considered as the uncreated word of God, revealed as such in the Qur'anic text. But to the extent to which the Qur'an repeats the content of the Abrahamic revelation, it can itself be considered as a revelation, as is the Old Testament. Furthermore, the Qur'an names itself *dhikr*, that is "reminder," in order to make it clear that the message it contains is a reminder of what God has already revealed to humankind from the time of Abraham, and even before that. The Qur'anic text can therefore be regarded by Christians as the human expression of the prophetic mission of Muhammad. Speaking of the Qur'an, Dupuis affirms that "this revelation is neither perfect nor complete; for all that, it is nevertheless real.[33] The declaration of the Congregation for the Doctrine of the Faith, *Dominus Iesus*, teaches that "[t]he sacred books of other religions, which in actual fact direct and nourish the existence of their followers, receive from the mystery of Christ the elements of goodness and grace which they contain."[34]

It is clear that for the Christian, a recognition of the prophetic character of Muhammad and of the Qur'anic message rest upon the extent to which they are party to the Abrahamic covenant, which has nothing contradictory in itself to the revelation in Jesus Christ. In other words, even if Islam is later than Christianity in terms of history, it is to be perceived theologically, in the plan of the covenant, as preceding it.

Islam therefore constitutes for the Christian a kind of prophecy in permanence, which recalls Christians to the Abrahamic foundation of their faith. This calls Christians to abide – not without difficulty – in the adoration and the mystery of the One God, the God of Abraham and of our ancestors while at the same time invoking the same God as Father, Son, and Holy Spirit. Further, and in the sense in which the Muslim religion is a constant reminder of the "verticality" of human life, which only has meaning in the attitude of prostrating oneself permanently before God – as in the five daily prayers – Christians may learn from Muslims not to dilute the Christian message, founded on the closeness of God to us through the Incarnation, into a simple horizontal ethic of life and loving fellowship. Blessed Charles de Foucauld recognized that it is thanks to the witness of Muslims practicing their daily prayers, encountered in Morocco, that he recovered the faith and consecrated himself to live out the Gospel among Muslims, in an attitude of adoration and universal friendship (fraternité universelle).

Furthermore, the particular recognition which Christianity may have for Islam challenges the Qur'anic message on two levels. On the one hand, with regard to the exaggerated legalism which dominates in Islam today, transforming the religion into a simple code of life and a slavish imitation of the salafs (the elders, i.e., the first three generations of Muslims), the gospel message may be a reminder to Muslims of the centrality of the relationship with God in the Abrahamic faith. This faith is expressed in an attitude of inner abandonment to divine providence and of compassion toward others, rather than in an external ritualism.

There is as well a reciprocal theological questioning between Christianity and Islam regarding the definition of the person of Christ and his mission. Certainly, Christians have an interest and respect for the particular place that the Qur'an gives to Christ and to his mother Mary. The theological divergences nevertheless remain an open question, and an inevitable challenge. In so far as Islam places itself in chronological time, it risks abandoning its exemplary spiritual role in order to enter into a logic of fulfilment or of correction of the Jewish and Christian revelations which preceded it. From this perspective, I ask myself whether Muslims may not be led to recognize in the Bible – Old and New Testaments – a kind of Old Testament to the Qur'anic message. Thus the Qur'an only reveals its whole meaning in the light of the Jewish and Christian traditions, even if for the Muslim, the Gospels and the Torah must in turn be interpreted by means of the Qur'anic message.

This approach encourages theologians to replace apologetics by a theology in dialogue, which on the one hand takes account of the relation between the two faiths and their claim to universality, and on the other, the oneness of God and the coherence of his divine plan. It is certainly a delicate exercise, which can only succeed if it is guided by the light which comes from engagement with spirituality and divine wisdom.

Such an approach to theological dialogue may prompt a questioning for Islam and encourage a reflection on its readings and interpretations of the Qur'anic text. Some Muslim thinkers recognize, for example, that while upholding belief in the authenticity of Qur'anic revelation, it is not wrong to consider the Qur'anic text as a product of history marked by its socio-cultural context. They themselves call for a less literalist reading of the text and an interpretation which gives room for historico-critical studies.[35]

The New Covenant in Jesus Christ

With Jesus Christ, the fullness of the revelation of God for human beings, Christians believe humanity is brought into a new covenant which recapitulates, decisively and definitively, the two preceding covenants, the Adamic and the Abrahamic. Jesus is therefore not the founder of Christianity, but rather the "re-founder" of the covenant of God with the whole of creation, through whom God will be all in all (cf. 1 Cor. 15:28). For, as the apostle Paul states, in Jesus Christ "dwells the fullness of divinity" (Col. 2:9). Thus from the Christian point of view, it is fundamental not to think of Christ only as the Messiah of Israel, but as the new Adam who recapitulates in himself the whole of creation and the covenants and brings time to its conclusion. Furthermore, the third and new covenant with Christ is not just the simple renewal or fulfilment of the two covenants, the Adamic and Abrahamic which preceded him. While he is the new Adam and the Messiah who fulfils in his own person all the promises of the covenant with the Jewish people, Jesus Christ represents also the decisive and fullest revelation of God for the whole of humanity.

Thus, according to the Epistle to the Hebrews, "Long ago God spoke to our ancestors in many and various ways by the prophets, but in these last days he has spoken to us by a Son, whom he appointed heir of all things, through whom he also created the worlds" (Heb. 1:1-2). This verse places the coming of Jesus Christ in a particular phase of history that it calls "the last days," while at the same time placing the person of Christ at the origin of time as creator and at the end as the heir. St. John describes him as being the alpha and omega of history (cf. Rev. 21:6). For this reason, the Second Vatican Council considered that this new covenant "will never pass away, and no new public revelation is to be expected before the glorious manifestation of our Lord, Jesus Christ (cf. 1Tim. 6:14 and Titus 2:13)" (*Dei Verbum* 4).

While full and definitive, this revelation, according to Dupuis, is not, however, absolute. The fact that no revelation, either before or after Christ, is able to surpass or equal that which has been accorded in Jesus Christ "does not hinder, even after the historic event, a divine revelation of a personal kind continued by the prophets and sages of other religious traditions."[36] For, as affirmed by the document of the International Theological Commission, *Christianity and the World Religions,* "God gives himself to be known and continues to give himself to be known to human beings in diverse ways."[37]

Thus we see that the words of Vatican II on the end of all public revelation are found to be nuanced with regard to the understanding of the fullness of revelation, not in quantitative terms but rather in qualitative ones: it is not a question of knowing in theory who is the last of the prophets, but of recognizing him by the way in which he fulfils all of the prophecies and of which he is the origin. Furthermore, in the messianic times which inaugurate the Christian Pentecost, prophecy becomes a universal gift (cf. Acts 2:17).

Christ, the fullness of revelation

The fullness of the Christian revelation is to be understood in a sense both qualitative and eschatological. For those who believe in him, the eternal Word of God, Jesus Christ cannot be placed in parallel or in concurrence with any other prophet or founder of religion. Rather, he is perceived as being the source of all divine revelation. Christ represents, as it were, the mystery of God "in whom are hidden all the treasures of wisdom and knowledge" (Col. 2:3). It is in this sense that the Christian revelation is considered qualitatively, and not quantitatively, full and complete, for the Word of God is no stranger to any authentic revelation. As a result, the Christian revelation cannot be considered the only truth. Rather, it constitutes the fullness of the truth that is disseminated in all the other revelations.

The revelation in Christ is equally complete eschatologically, that is to say that it brings human history into "God's time." The authors of the New Testament insist on the idea that with the coming of Jesus Christ "the time is fulfilled" (Mark 1:15). However, this idea was not easy to understand and to explain to the first believers. The fulfilment of time was linked to the presence of Christ, and so to his imminent return after his resurrection. Thus the apostle Paul seems to believe that this return will not be delayed in being accomplished, even in his own lifetime (cf. 1 Thess. 4:13-18; 2 Thess. 2:1-12). Christians are to live motivated by the expectation of this return, always in their prayer. And so the New Testament concludes with this invocation: "Amen, come Lord Jesus!" (Rev. 22:20). The history of humanity is in this way suspended between its own time and that of God, and overlaps with those times which are the last. It is as if from now onwards, time is on countdown to the end, and everything is interpreted in the light of this same end. And it is thusly that Christianity regards other religions, as they are also pulled toward this same end, where Christ will become all in all.

The cosmic Christ and the seeds of the Word

The whole history of salvation and of the revelation of God for humanity is made clear, therefore, by the mystery of Christ that embraces all beings, from the creation until the Parousia. Jesus Christ, therefore, is no stranger to the covenants which precede the new covenant of the New Testament, or even to what follows. Monsignor Georges Khodr, Greek Orthodox Archbishop of Mount Lebanon, affirms that "[t]he Logos is not exhausted by becoming incarnate."[38] For this reason he suggests a rehabilitation of the patristic theology of the *logos spermatikos,* in order to discover and to "awake the Christ who sleeps in the night of the religions"[39] Monsignor Joseph Doré, former Catholic archbishop of Strasbourg, for his part calls for the recognition of an active work of Christ (*"function christique"*) within the non-Christian religions themselves. He suggests that their ways of acting and living, with the rules and the doctrines which constitute religions, may be considered as fruits of the Spirit of Christ. They "will therefore be, as a result, the means of the action – and also of the presence – of Christ within and even through the non-Christian religions."[40]

Taking up the patristic metaphor of "seeds of the Word," Vatican II asks Christians to become familiar with the national and religious traditions of their fellow citizens, and to "discover with joy and respect the seeds of the Word which they find hidden there" (*Ad gentes* 11). This dissemination of seeds of the Word, across epochs and nations, reminds us that God who creates and sustains all things by the Word (cf. John 1:3), takes constant care of the human race, in order to give eternal life to all those who, by their faithfulness to that which is good, seek for salvation (cf. *Dei Verbum* 3).

Explaining to the Roman curia the event of the interreligious gathering in Assisi of 2 October 1986, of which he was the initiator, Pope John Paul II reflected on this mystery of the unity of humanity, even of religions, in the Word of God using very strong terms and which are worth quoting in their entirety.[41] "In the light of the mystery, differences of every kind, and in the first place religious differences, to the extent that they are reductive of the plan of God, show themselves in effect as belonging to another order. If the order of unity goes back to creation and redemption, and is in this sense 'divine', these differences and divergences – even the religions ones – go back rather to a 'human fact' [a 'condition belonging to humanity'] and must be overtaken in the progress toward the realisation of the great plan of unity which oversees creation." The pope's words build on the conciliar declaration on the relations of the church with non-Christian religions, *Nostra aetate*, which, in its preamble, affirms that all peoples form one single community, having a single origin and the same final destiny: God himself.

The text adds that God helps all human beings without exception on their path of life toward him, by his providence, his actions of kindness, and his plans of salvation (cf. *Nostra aetate* 1). Following on from this, the pope distinguishes between divergences and divisions which reflect human limitations and obstruct the fundamental unity of human beings according to the plan of God, and the differences which reflect the distinctive qualities and the spiritual riches given by God to the nations. Thus, even when they profess religious truths which are incompatible with those held by others and feel that their differences are insurmountable, human beings remain, nevertheless, included in the great and unique plan of God in Jesus Christ. On this basis, John Paul II did not hesitate to see in the ecumenical and interreligious day of prayer at Assisi the visible expression, if only for an instant, of "the unity, hidden and yet radical, that the divine Word has established between men and women of this world."[42]

Christ, Christianity, and the others

The discrepancy between the inclusiveness of the universal mystery of Christ and the limits of Christianity as one historic religion among many others constitutes a great paradox for Christian theology, of which the sacramentality of the church in its relation to the kingdom is the only pathway to achieving greater clarity. The church is in the service of a reality which transcends it, while being called to be a sign of this reality. "Working for the Kingdom" means therefore, according to Pope John Paul II, "acknowledging and promoting God's activity, which is present in human history and transforms it. Building the kingdom means working for liberation from evil in all its forms. In a word, the kingdom of God is the manifestation and the realization of God's plan of salvation in all its fullness."[43]

In the dogmatic constitution on the church, *Lumen gentium*, Vatican II declared that the church is, in Christ, "a sacrament – a sign and instrument, that is, of communion with God and of the unity of the whole human race" (*Lumen gentium* 1). In consequence, the same conciliar text affirms further on, "Finally, those who have not yet received the Gospel, are in various ways appointed (*Lat. ordianantur*) to the people of God" (*Lumen gentium* 16). The church is therefore in the service of God's plan to gather all his children into a unity between themselves and with him. Following Christ's example, the church may not consider itself in concurrence with other religions. Rather, it is called to be the reason for their journey in unity toward the fullness of divine blessings.

John Paul II considered that the Day of Assisi, in its interreligious dimension, gives an illustration of "the real and objective value of this 'ordination' to the unity of the unique People of God, often hidden from our eyes."[44] This event became for the pope a kind of archetype of the conscience that the church should have regarding itself and its mission among other religions. This mission begins, first of all, with recognition and respect of this "ordination" of others to the people of God, and there being a mysterious relationship, brought about by God, between these persons and the unity of the people of

God. Secondly, the church is called by means of *diakonia* (service) to promote unity, charity, and reconciliation between human beings, after the example of its master and founder who offered his life, not only for his nation, "but to gather into one the dispersed children of God" (John 11:52)

The visitation of Mary to Elizabeth is an inspiring example and an allegory of the relationship that the church is called live in with other religions (cf. Luke 1:39-56). Mary, who carries in her womb the Word of God who is made flesh of her own flesh, represents the church, which is the mystical body of Christ and which carries him within herself for today's world, wherever she finds herself. Elizabeth for her part, wife of Zechariah, priest in the Temple of God in Jerusalem, the centre of Jewish religious life, carries in herself John, the great and last of the prophets of the Mosaic covenant. It is he who will one day baptize Jesus and call his people to conversion (cf. Luke 3:3). At that time, Mary did not know the link between the two infants. Christian de Chergé interprets this passage in the light of Islamic–Christian relations, saying, "We know that those whom we are called to encounter, they are a little like Elizabeth, they are bearers of a message which comes from God. And our Church does not tell us and does not know what is the exact link between the Good News that we are carrying and this message which gives life to the other.... I go to the Muslims," he concludes, "without knowing what is this link."[45]

The choice of Mary, the "mother of God," to come and live with Elizabeth for three months in order to help her during her pregnancy is an important lesson of humility, and also of faithfulness to the grace of God. In response to Mary's initiative, Elizabeth recognized in her the one blessed above all women, and also the holy infant in her womb. If one accepts the allegorical dimension to this text, then the way that the church, after the example of Mary, will be proclaimed blessed by all the nations and generations, and that Jesus will be recognized as the blessed one of God, can here be clearly discerned.

The church is called to be in "situations of visitation" in relation to other religious communities. In other words, the church is invited to take the initiative in order to reduce the distance which separates it from others, like Mary who left her home in Nazareth in Galilee in haste so as to be with Elizabeth in her home town in Judea. The Church, represented by its pastors, the faithful, and its local communities, is called in mission to approach "the others" and dwell with them, to be of service to them, for they bear within themselves "divine seeds" and a "prophetic voice." In this way, interreligious relationships become real occasions of "Magnificat," of praise for the name of God.

As I conclude this chapter, I would emphasize both the universality and generosity that are characteristic of the merciful love of God toward humanity. God has not created human beings in order to judge them, but to love them and share with them God's divine life. The covenants are truly an expression of this unquenchable love, described by the prophet Hosea under the form of betrothal. Love is in reality the key by which the relationship of God with the world and with human beings may be interpreted. Thanks to the very nature of divine love and of divine faithfulness, all covenants are irrevocable. From the Christian perspective, this gives meaning to the death of Christ on the cross, the gift of his life in pure love for all human beings and in faithfulness to them and to his Father.

4. ISLAM AND OTHER RELIGIONS

Nayla Tabbara

Religions in the Qur'an

The religions mentioned by their names in the Qur'an are not many: Christianity, Judaism, Sabianism and the religion of the Magians. Christianity and Judaism are referred to throughout the Qur'an, whether under their specific titles *yahud* (Jews) and *nasara* (Nazareans), or under a common appellation: *Ahl al Kitab* (people of the Book). Sabianism or Sabians (*sabi'a*) are by contrast only mentioned twice[1] and the religion of the Magians (*majus*) only once.[2]

It is quite difficult to define Sabianism as this name has been given to several groups: first to the followers of John the Baptist, who still exist in our days; second to philosophers inspired, according to Mas'udi, by Platonic and Neo-platonic doctrines to which they had added an astral cult; third to gnostics who associated with Neoplatonic doctrines, some texts of Hermes Trismegistus, and a veneration for Seth, third son of Adam. The Jewish scholar Moses Maimonides affirmed that the Sabians possess a book attributed to Adam, a book attributed to Seth, and a book attributed to Hermes (who, in Muslim tradition, corresponds to Idris, the Qur'anic prophet who is identified with the biblical Enoch).[3]

The identification of the Magians is very simple, Muslims having quickly identified them with Zoroastrians *(mazdeans)*, devotees of the dominant religion in Iran at the period of the conquests, the religion founded by Zoroaster and which has a book, the *Avesta*. While considered a dualist religion because of its portrayal of the universe as a combat zone between good and evil, that is between Ahura Mazda (Ohrmazd) and Ahriman, the faithful of this religion refer to explain it as philosophically dualist, but theologically monotheist.

The Qur'an also mentions, without giving them specific names, polytheistic religions of antiquity or of the period of the birth of Islam. Thus we find mentioned Meccan polytheism, called "associationism" from the fact that in this form of worship there were three kinds of divinities associated with God (Allah): chthonic divinities (related to the earth or underworld), astral divinities, and angels and demons considered as divine. The Qur'an mentions three among these divinities: Lat, Uzza and Manat, feminine divinities considered in the Meccan pantheon as daughters of Allah.[4] Some identify Allat with Aphrodite or Minerva, and al Uzza with Venus, while the Qur'an itself seems to indicate that these divinities were considered at one and the same time as three feminine angels and as daughters of Allah.[5]

At the same level as the polytheistic religion of the Meccans, the Qur'an mentions the religion of ancient Egypt, referring to two episodes: first to the time of Moses, with the Pharaoh who claimed to be a god, but who ended by believing in the God of Moses and his fathers, proclaiming himself to be a Muslim[6] (*Yunus* 10.90); and then to the time of Joseph, who spoke to his companions in prison as follows: "You only worship, apart from Him, some names that you have invented – you and your ancestors – and in response to which God has not sent down any proof. Power (*hukm*) belongs only to God. He has commanded you to worship none but Him. This is the right religion, but most people do not know it" (*Yusuf* 12.40). The same question of names invented by humans for gods is taken up again in the Qur'an with the polytheists of Mecca[7] and also with the people of Ad, an ancient Arabian people to whom an Arab prophet named Hud had been sent.[8] Finally, the Qur'an mentions, in connection with the story of Abraham, the religion of Nimrod and the people of Ur, in other words the religion of the Sumerians.[9]

We should note that apart from their "associationism" or polytheism and their invention of divinities, the Qur'an criticizes the social dimension of inequality displayed by the rich and tyrants belonging to these religions, as well as the arrogance of their representatives.

We also note that, among the religions mentioned in the Qur'an, it is only the Christian and Jewish religions, called religions of "the people of the Book" (*Ahl al Kitab*), who benefit from a special title that is used regularly. The other religions have been allotted, or deprived of, or considered close to the title *Ahl al Kitab* according to circumstance. The Zoroastrians have been considered people of the Book thanks to the *Avesta*, except that intermarriage with Muslims has always been forbidden to them. The Sabians were considered as people of the Book for some time, but this title was withdrawn from them when the Muslims discovered their astral cult.

This chapter will therefore concentrate mostly on the people of the Book, as well as on the Qur'anic account and view of the Meccan polytheists. In the latter part, we will widen our consideration to include other religions of yesterday and today.

Islam and the people of the Book

During the 23 years of the prophetic mission, the Qur'anic revelation accompanied the developing community with what we may call a vertical and a horizontal way. Vertically, it reminded the community of God's unicity, of divine closeness, of the balance and of the return to God; horizontally it addressed, with the new community, the various contextual, historic, geographical, political, and social demands and requirements. Aziz Esmail suggests that the Qur'an is "an ongoing, open-ended, evolving, self-revising commentary on, and a response to the situation and events in the Hijaz."[10] Thus it is in following the chronological order of the Qur'anic discourse concerning "the other" that we may gain an idea of the theology of other religions in Islam.

The chronology of the Qur'an is generally divided into two major periods, the Meccan period, which extends from the beginning of the mission (around 609 CE) until 622, and the Medinan period, extending from 622, the date of the emigration of the Prophet and his companions to Medina, until 632, the year in which Muhammad died. Each of these two periods has its own character.

Islam in Mecca is an Islam of new converts, persecuted, dreaming of a world of justice and without oppression, and confronting with patience and endurance the persecutions on the part of the Meccans. It is a purely Abrahamic Islam, *hanif*, without laws, almost without practices of its own. And, like Abraham who rose up against the gods of his people, risking his life[11] and breaking with his environment and its beliefs by emigrating to a new land, the new Muslim community left Mecca for Yathrib – rebaptized Medina – which signified "the town," namely the town of the Prophet.

There, the adherents to the new faith found themselves in a situation of security, as if they had reached a promised land, but yet to realize that all is not for the best even in the best of worlds. They were no more persecuted or banished or subjected to a boycott, but they were up against communities of believers they considered to be allies, but who did not give them the recognition they had expected.

In fact, transplanted to Medina, and placed in daily contact with the Jewish tribes of the town and with the Christians of the region, the idealism of the Meccan Islam saw itself diminished and faded away. We can feel at this point a tension in the Qur'an between on the one hand a demand to be accepted by others - by the people of the Book – and, on the other hand, an appeal to blend in the three religions (Jewish, Christian, and the faith of Muhammad's followers) to form a monotheism situated in the middle between the two religions of Judaism and Christianity, to which would be added faith in Muhammad as messenger. This monotheism of the middle ground called for belief in all the biblical prophets and patriarchs, adding to Judaism faith in Jesus as having been sent by God, as a sign and as Messiah, but withdrawing from the Christian beliefs in the Incarnation and divine Sonship. Now began those permanent negotiations through which, faced with the clearly separate identities of the Jews of Medina and the Christians of Arabia, notably of *Najran*, Islam tried to form its proper identity and its own symbols within the line of the economy of the Reminder. This coincided with the putting in place of practices and laws which became characteristic of an Islam that was taking a more defined form than had previously existed. But tension remained, particularly between a desire for unity on the one hand, and the necessity of accepting diversity on the other.

Before moving on to consider the successive phases of the relations between the first Muslims and the people of the Book according to the Qur'anic chronology, I wish to recall that the Qur'an makes use of two forms of discourse in relation to the people of the Book. The first is narrative, comprising the biblical accounts, and the second is dialogical, the Qur'an addressing itself in this case directly to the people of the Book using the expression "O people of the Book." The Meccan period is full of the first kind of discourse, a Qur'anic reminder of the biblical narratives concerning the patriarchs and prophets, while the Medinan period is by comparison dialogical.

The Meccan Period and the Unity of Believers

In the *surahs* of the first period, which contain the biblical narratives, the Qur'an addresses itself to the growing community in order to explain that it is but one, fundamentally, with the two other communities of Jews and of Christians. The *surah al Anbiya'* (the Prophets), for example, after having recounted some parts of the stories concerning Moses, Aaron, Abraham, Lot, Noah, David, Solomon, Jonah, Zechariah, John, and then Mary adds "in truth this community is yours, and it is one community. I am your Lord! Worship me therefore!" (*Al Anbiya'* 21.92). It seems therefore that the Qur'anic instruction wants to instil from the beginning in the hearts of the members of the new community, a desire for unity with all the religions of the reminder. However the Qur'an adds immediately afterward: "They have instigated schisms among themselves, but all will return to Us," *(Al Anbiya'* 21.93), as if to indicate that unity is there, but it is marked by internal dissensions.

The same dynamic is to be found in another *surah* of the same Meccan period, where, following the mention of Noah, Moses, Jesus and Mary, two verses follow, one relevant to unity, the other deploring division: "This community of yours is truly one and the same community, and I, I am your Lord! Fear me therefore! But men are divided into sects, each faction celebrating that which separates it" *(Al Mu'minun* 23.52-53). Diversity is therefore not perceived positively at this stage but depicted as a schism caused by the self-preoccupation of each group within the same broad community of believers.

Toward the end of the Meccan period, another form of discourse with the people of the Book becomes apparent. A verse which anticipates later dialogue instructs the growing community on how to address the people of the Book: "And do not dispute which is the best way with the people of the Book, except with those who are unjust. And say 'we believe in that which has been sent down to us and sent down to you, for your God and our God is the same, and it is to Him that we submit ourselves'" *(Al Ankabut* 29.46).

God instructs the Muslims, therefore, to represent themselves to the people of the Book as forming part of the same economy of the Reminder, the same revelation and as believing in the same God.

The Medinan Period

Islam encounters religious specifities

All the other verses recording discourse with the people of the Book belong to the Medinan period. They begin with the *surah al Baqara*, the first Medinan *surah*. There, we find a negotiation within the same *surah*. The first reference to the people of the Book is the promise of salvation (2.62). "Surely, those who believe, those who practice Judaism, those who are Christians or Sabians, whoever believes in God and in the last Day and practices righteousness, these will find their reward with their Lord and they will not undergo fear or affliction" (*Al Baqara* 2.62). The absence of fear and affliction mentioned in these verses, refers to the moment of the last Judgment, and implies that salvation is promised to the followers of those religions that are mentioned, and "whoever believes in God, in the Last Day and does good deeds,"[12] whoever follows, knowing it or not, the way of Islam in the broad sense.

However, probably in response to the refusal on the part of the Jewish tribes of Medina to recognize the Message of Muhammad as a continuation of the same revelation, the *surah* moves on quickly to put forward verses of a different tone.

From the dream of unity to the "schism"

We find, therefore, in the first Medinan *surah*, *Al Baqara*, two reactions on the part of the people of the Book, with regard to the developing religion: on the one hand, non-recognition: "When a messenger of God has come to them confirming what they have already received, a party of those to whom the Book has been delivered reject, behind their backs, the Book of God, as if they know nothing" (*Al Baqara* 2.101); on the other hand, a recognition of the message of Muhammad, expressed in the Qur'an which gives praise to this reaction: "Those to whom We have given the Book, who recite it as it requires, those believe in it" (*Al Baqara* 2.121). The difference at this stage is therefore between individuals and not at the level of the communities, which we can infer from the Qur'anic policy of not making generalizing statements, but rather using such expressions as "a portion of," "a number of," "a group among them," and "a party of them."

It follows in relation to the same theme, the Qur'anic message puts forward a denunciation of the amalgamation between religious identity and faith, and of the religious competition between Jews and Christians:

> They have said: "No-one will enter Paradise unless they be a Jew or a Christian." Such is their mistaken hope. Say: "Bring forward your

proof if you are truthful." Surely, whoever submits himself to God and does good will have his reward with his Lord… He will not suffer fear or affliction. The Jews say, "The Christians stand on nothing!" The Christians say, "The Jews stand on nothing!" while they all read the Book. Those who know nothing speak similarly. God will judge between them on the day of Resurrection and He will decide regarding their differences. (*Al Baqqara* 2.111-113).

The message at this period therefore calls for interreligious rivalry to be overcome by a reminder of what is at the heart of faith, notably faith in God and well-doing.

The issue of competition is linked to the question of the alteration of the Divine Word, an issue also taken up by the *surah Al Baqara,* in a dialogue which begins by being critical toward the people of the Book: "How can you wish these people to believe you when a party among them has heard the Word of God, then has altered it secretly after having understood it" *(Al Baqara* 2.75). While it is evident that the alteration means here an alteration in the sense of bias in interpretation given by "a party among them" (the children of Israel), the author of the first full commentary on the Qur'an, Tabari (d. 310 H/922), gives two interpretations of this verse: first, that of *tahrif al ma'na,* alteration of the sense and not of the text itself, and second, which does not fit the context of the first part of the Medinan period but rather the climate of polemical treatises of the epoch Tabari himself, treatises of refutation of the Jewish and Christian religions and of the demonstration of the superiority of Islam. According to this second interpretation, some Jewish scholars have altered, that is erased, some sections of the Torah which mentioned the Prophet Muhammad.[13]

Abdelmajid Charfi notes that another Tabari, Ali ibn Rabban at-Tabari (d. approx. 241H/ 855), a Christian convert to Islam, in an approach bringing together the two interpretations, tried to collect fragments of the Old and New Testament that would have mentioned Muhammad as in the verse concerning, "Those who follow the Messenger, the *ummi* (gentile) Prophet, whom they will find inscribed in their Torah and Gospel (*Injil*)" (*Al A'raf* 7.157). It seems that most of these instances, according to Charfi, are "what it is usual to call 'messianic texts' in which Christians have seen references to Jesus, and which are reinterpreted in such a way that they can be applied to Muhammad." Charfi remarks that these passages or fragments collected by Ali at-Tabari form the foundation which all later Muslims who address this matter rely on. He develops his reflection on this further: "The phenomenon inaugurated by Tabari is interesting in the measure to which the Old Testament has been interpreted by Christians in the light of the New, and that the one and the other have been reinterpreted in the light of the Qur'an by Muslims. We have there a striking example of the application of the same method of approach to the Scriptures."[14]

I would add that we are here dealing with the same kind of blame, the Muslims blaming the Christians and the Jews in the same way that the Christians reproach their predecessors in monotheistic faith. The difference, however, is that the Christians have kept the Jewish Bible as Scripture, while the Muslims have not made the Bible a part of their Scripture by considering the Jewish and Christian scriptures as an Old Testament to the Qur'an.

Returning to the consideration of the chronology of the Qur'an, we notice that, with regard to all these reproaches of non-recognition, of concurrence between religions and alteration of meaning, the Qur'an does not respond yet with a strict definition of Muslim identity, but continues to speak of a religion of submission to God and of well-doing. In other terms, it maintains, at the beginning of the Medinan period, the idea of, and the appeal to an Islam in a broad sense. "Neither Jews nor Christians will be content with you while you do not follow their religion Say: God's guidance is the [only true] guidance" (*Al Baqara* 2.120), or again, "They have said, 'Be Jews or Christians, you will then be in the right way." - Say: 'No, but we follow the religion of Abraham, the true model of righteousness and who was never one of the Associators'" (*Al Baqara* 2.135).

The message insists therefore on the unity of the people of the Book, that is Jews, Christians, and Muslims, in one and the same religion. But the differences between the Jews and the Christians with the Muslims and between themselves seem to provide an obstacle to this unity. Thus God continues to instruct the followers of Muhammad to take up and put forward again their proposal for the unification in an Islam in the broad sense, while adding at the same time that if the receivers of this proposal reject it, the members of the developing community will have no other option but to consider them as schismatics:

> Say, "We believe in God, in that which has been revealed to us, in that which was revealed to Abraham, to Ishmael, to Isaac, to Jacob and to the tribes; in that which has been given to Moses and to Jesus; in that which has been given to the prophets coming from their Lord. We do not make any difference between them; we are submitted to Him." If they believe in what you believe, they are well guided; but if they turn away, they are now in schism. God will suffice for you against them; He is the Hearer, the Knower. *(Al Baqara 2.136 -137)*

And, as it happened, the Qur'anic negotiation and appeal to this unique religion did not achieve its aims. The schism is then brought about, and Islam in the narrower sense begins. The first symbol of this autonomy of Islam with regard to its faithful is the direction of the prayer. The Muslims had prayed until now in the direction of Jerusalem. Once it became evident that the people of the Book refused to unite in one Abrahamic religion, Islam went ahead to form its own proper identity, changing the direction of the prayer (*qibla*), and recovering a purely Abrahamic repertoire, pre-dating the two schisms with the Jews and the Christians. It chose, therefore, Mecca as *qibla*, for the Qur'an describes it as containing, in the Kaaba, the first place of prayer dedicated to God that was ever constructed, built by Abraham and Ishmael.[15]

From the schism to the establishment of the Muslim community

The first Medinan *surah* warns: "Even if you bring to those who have received the Book all possible signs, they will not follow your *Qibla*, and you will not follow their *Qibla*, any more than some of them will not follow the *Qibla* of others" *(Al Baqara 2.145)*. "For each being there is an orientation to which he turns. Compete therefore in good deeds. Wherever you are, God will join with you, and He will lead you all toward Himself" *(Al Baqara 2.148)*.

And so the marriage which Islam hoped for never took place. Nevertheless, the call is not to rise up against the other, but to accept the differences and to compete in good deeds, knowing that all are under the eye of God. Knowing also that salvation is offered to all who believe in God and in the last day, and who carry out good works, who follow the example of Abraham without, however, having to belong to his descendants. The Qur'an reminds us that salvation is not a question of religious identity or genetic inheritance: "Remember: when his Lord tested Abraham by certain orders and when he had accomplished them, God said to him: 'I am going to make of you an example for mankind.' 'And what of my descendants?' asked Abraham. The Lord replied, "My covenant does not extend to the unjust'" *(Al Baqara 2.124)*.

Even though the schism took place, and it seems that the differences had to be accepted as reality, at the same time the Qur'an never closes its arms and does not give up on its appeal for a unity based upon revelation. The appeal by word not having produced a result, it uses or calls for another approach, dear to the medieval world: discernment by means of a test or trial in order to ascertain the truth of a matter. This test (*mubahala*) was presented, according to commentators on the Qur'an, to the Christians of Najran, when they visited Medina and followed on from the welcome given to them by the Prophet in opening for them the mosque adjoining his house so that they might carry out their prayer. The circumstances which led from the welcome and hospitality to an invitation to accomplish the test are not altogether clear, nor is what followed from the issuing of this invitation.

Researchers have reached the conclusion that, in the event, the test was not carried out,[16] and the authors of the biography of the Prophet suggest that the Christians of Najran paid a tribute to Muhammad and then returned home. The matter of the tribute is not apparent in the Qur'anic text itself, but in some of the Qur'anic commentaries from the beginning of the third century of the Hijra (ninth century CE). This link made by commentators between the test and the tribute describes rather the practices at the time of the exegetes and hardly serves to clarify the episode of the test.

Then, whatever was the outcome of the story of the test—in other words whether it took place or not or was replaced by the payment of a tribute—the Qur'an continues its discourse directly with the people of the Book, with a fresh invitation to unite around a common word, which corresponds in fact to Islam in the broader sense: "Say: 'O people of the Book! Come and join around a word which we will have in common, for us and for you, that we should worship only God, that we should not associate anything with Him and that no-one among us should take lords apart from God.' If they turn away, say to them: 'Witness that we are those who submit!'"(*Al Imran* 3.64).

And the *surah* challenges the people of the Book with regard to Abraham: "O people of the Book! Why do you dispute on the subject of Abraham, when the Torah and the Gospel have only been revealed subsequent to him?" (*Al Imran* 3.65), and in reply to them: "Abraham was not a Jew nor a Christian, but he was a pure believer (*hanif*), submitted to God (*muslim*), not joining with the associationists" (*Al Imran* 3.67).

While this appeal continued to be restated, despite the schism in the Abrahamic faith, the *surah*s of the Medinan period contain two elements at this stage concerning the people of the Book, an admonition concerning their deviations from the two primordial covenants, and a reproach regarding the non-recognition, even the opposition, to the message of Muhammad.

Concerning the non-recognition, it seems to have developed and shifted into blatant adversity: "Say: 'O people of the Book! Why do you make an obstacle for the believer on the way of God and would you wish that this way should be difficult, of which you are witnesses?' But God is not oblivious to what you do" (*Al Imran* 3.99). For this reason a kind of separation is demanded for Muslims on the part of God. This separation is not applicable, however, to all the people of the Book but concerns a party of them, probably the most aggressive toward the new community: "O you who believe! If you obey a group of those who have received the Scriptures, they will make of you offenders after you have received the faith" (*Al Imran* 3.99). The Qur'an persists in not "generalizing" and to make clear that its disagreement is not with a whole community but with individuals who show by their attitude, not only a hostility and an ill will toward Islam, but also an infidelity with regard to their own religion.

For this reason, and because in itself it acts as guarantor of the pacts between God and human beings, the Qur'an admonishes the people of the Book concerning the preservation of these pacts, and praises those who respect them. It recalls, for example, the breaking of the pact with God on the part of a group among the people of the Book in ignoring God's signs and killing the prophets, while it underlines that others are among the righteous:

They are not all the same: there exists among the people of the Book, a righteous community whose members recite the verses of God during the night and prostrate themselves. They believe in God and the last Day, they observe what is correct, they forbid what is to be condemned, they compete in good deeds. These are among the righteous. Whatever good they accomplish, it will not be denied for them, for God knows perfectly the pious. *(Al Imran* 3.113-115)

Concerning the balance, it also states:

Among the people of the Book, is the one to whom you have entrusted a sack of gold and who returns it to you, and there are others to whom you have entrusted a dinar and who will not return it even if you assail them continually. And this because they say: "We are committed to nothing so far as the gentiles are concerned!" In fact, they put forward lies concerning God and do so knowingly. *(Al Imran 3.75)*

Further, in this second phase of its relations with the people of the Book, the Qur'an raises the issue of disbelief (*kufr*):

> Those who have disbelieved among the people of the Book, also the "Associationists," do not cease to disbelieve until there comes to them the evident Proof, a Messenger, on the part of God, who recites to them from pure pages, in which are found prescriptions for perfect conduct. And those to whom the Book has been given are not divided until after the proof has come to them. However, it has only been commanded for them to worship God like sincere believers, following a straight path *(hunafa')* and to make the prayer and to give alms. Such is the religion of righteousness. *(Al Bayyina* 98.1-5)

The disbelief referred to here is not part of a total disbelief; in other words it does not consist of disbelief in God, but of a disbelief in one of his prophets, Muhammad, a disbelief held in common by the "associationists" and the people of the Book. Another *surah* of the same period, entitled *Al Imran*, also makes reference to the disbelief in one of the prophets of God, in this case Jesus: "God then said: 'O Jesus! I am going in truth to call you again to Myself, to raise you up to Me, to purify you from those who disbelieve, and to place those who have followed you above the evil-doers until the Day of Resurrection. Soon you will return to Me; I will judge then between you and I will pronounce on your differences'" (*Al Imran* 3.55).

We must note that a certain shift in interpretation has taken place during the history of Islam with regard to the Qur'anic terminology. The Qur'an is in fact consistent in its terminology, and only uses the terms "unbelievers" (*kuffar*) and "associationists" (*mushrikin*) for the

Meccan polytheists. And when it refers to a "non-faith" on the part of the people of the Book with regard to one aspect or another of the Muslim message, it uses the expression "those who have disbelieved," but never calls the people of the Book "the unbelievers" or "the associationists." Certain Muslim preachers, however, ignore this and apply these two terms to the people of the Book, altering thus the meaning and the interpretation with regard to the Qur'anic message.

At this second phase of the Medinan period, around the third year of the Hijra, the Muslims marked themselves out in various ways as distinct from the people of the Book, and established the Muslim community in the restricted sense. Until then, the early community in Medina was a mixed community, containing Muslims and Jews. The constitution of Medina,[17] called also "The Document of the Umma," was drawn up in the first year of the Hijra in order to regulate relations between the Muslim immigrants (called Qurayshis, as they come from the Quraysh tribe) and the people of Yathrib-Medina, thus among Muslims, Jews of Medina and theose who were tied to both by pacts. This constitution affirms: "The Jews make up one community with the believers."[18] Verse 104 of the third *surah, Al Imran*, may also refer to this mixed community of believers: "Let there be among you one community whose members support righteousness, commanding what is acceptable and forbidding what is worthy of condemnation. Those are the successful ones!"

Then, in the third year of the Hijra, the Muslim community began to recognize itself as a community apart from its neighbours. And God encouraged and comforted the growing community, who became a religion in the full meaning of the term, proclaiming its distinctness: "You are the best Community which has been established for human beings: you command that which is acceptable, you forbid that which should be condemned and you believe in God If the people of the Book believe, it will be better for them. There are believers among them, but for the most part they are schismatics" *(Al Imran* 3.110).

From a historical point of view, therefore, this interlude of negotiations with the people of the Book, the ensuing tensions, and the refusal on their part to unite together in one Abrahamic faith, aided the formation of Islam in the more restricted sense, and Islam became an autonomous religion.

Political and Religious Quarrels

Following this separation and development of Islam in the restricted sense, the Qur'an gives an account of the religious quarrels between Muslims, Christians, and Jews under three heads: dogmatic, ethical, and purely contextual and political.

At the political level, and therefore at the heart of the contextual, we have now arrived at a third phase in the relations between the first Muslims and the people of the Book, a phase characterized by an intensification of tensions, which led to conflict. This came about because a part of the people of the Book joined together with the Meccans against the Muslims, as we are informed in the *surah An Nisa'*: "Have you not noticed these people to whom a portion of the Scripture has been given? They believe in sorcery and in false gods (the *Taghut*), and they say of the wrongdoers: 'These are better guides on the way than the believers'" (*An Nisa'* 4.51). It is interesting to note that, when it addresses a significant deviation from the original pact, the Qur'an replaces the expression "people of the Book" with "those to whom a portion of the book has been given," showing that they were not worthy of the title "people of the Book."

The *surah* which follows, the *surah al Hashr*, describes the tensions with the Jewish tribe of Banu an-Nadir of Medina, in the fourth year of the Hijra. This tribe was not only allied to the Meccans but it was intriguing, from within Medina, against Muhammad. The danger for the Muslim community was both from the exterior and the interior, and therefore Muhammad and his supporters laid siege to the Banu an-Nadir entrenched in their fortresses. Following 11 days of the siege, the Banu an-Nadir surrendered and were sent into exile. The *surah* recounts:

It is He who has made to leave their homes, at the first mustering, those people of the Book who had given proof of their misdoings. You did not think that they would leave, and they thought that their fortresses would protect them against God. But God has surprised them in a way beyond their expectation, and he has thrown panic into their hearts. They have demolished their houses with their own hands and with those of the believers. Take from this a lesson, you who are so clear-sighted! If God had not decreed their banishment, he would certainly have punished them in this world. *(Al Hashr* 59.2-3)

The last section of this verse seems to me like a response to the questions of those Muslims who had not understood why these things had to reach this stage.

This exile was followed, in the fifth year, by a battle between the Muslims on the side and the Meccans in coalition with the other Jews of Medina on the other. The battle, named Al Khandaq (battle of the Trench) is described in *surah Al Ahzab* (the Confederates): "God has sent away those who disbelieved with their anger; they have obtained nothing good; God has sustained the believers in the battle; God is strong and powerful. He made descend from their strongholds those of the people of the Book who were to rally with them. He has thrown panic into their hearts. You have killed one part of them, and you have reduced to other to captivity" *(Al Ahzab* 33.25 -26).

At the same time, during the battles on two fronts against the Meccans and against the Medinans who had allied with them, a third element revealed itself: the discovery of hypocrites inside the ranks, described in brief in the *surah Al Ahzab*, but in more detail in the *surah* which carries their name, *Al Munafiqun* (the hypocrites): "They have made their oaths as a safeguard, but they are apart from the way of God. Surely, what they have done is detestable. It is particularly so, because they have believed and then disbelieved. A seal has then been placed on their hearts with the result that they do not know how to reason." *(Al Munafiqun* 62.2-3). In effect they were Muslims who had apostasized interiorly, while continuing to proclaim themselves to be Muslims, and who attempted to undermine the community from within, encouraging the followers of Muhammad to turn away from him: "These are the ones who say 'Do not worry about those who are loyal to the Messenger of God, for in the end they will leave him.' To God belongs the treasures of the heavens and of the earth, but the hypocrites do not know how to reason'"(*Al Munafiqun* 63.7).

We may note that these hypocrites exemplify, according to the Qur'an, the opposite way to that of faith, because they turn away from God and his Mercy and arm themselves with arrogance, breaking in that way the primordial covenant: "When one says to them: 'Come, the Messenger of God will ask forgiveness (from God) for you!' they turn away their heads and you see them withdrawing, puffed up with pride" (*Al Munafiqun* 63.5).

In the same direction, of increasing tensions and hostility, comes the *surah At-Tawba*, the most problematic *surah* in this respect, and the only Qur'anic *surah* which, enigmatically, does not begin with the formula "In the name of God, the Most Merciful, the Most Compassionate." This *surah* includes a verse which is known as "the verse of the sword." Extremists of yesterday and today claim that this one verse abrogates (annuls or replaces) all the other verses which mention the people of the Book and of which the tone is openness, recognition, and promise of salvation. For these extremists, this one verse abrogates in this way a quarter of the Qur'an.

Here is what the verse of the sword says: "Fight those who, among the people of the Book, do not believe in God nor the last Day, do not declare unlawful that which God and His Messenger has declared unlawful and do not practice the true Religion, and until they pay the tribute with their hands, making honourable amends" (*At Tawba* 9.29).

Historically, the circumstance of the revelation of this verse is not clear. Most of the sources attach it to a projected battle, at Tabuk in Syria, with Christian tribes, a battle which in fact did not take place according to the same sources. The sources add, however, that chief of the Christians of Syria paid a tribute to the Muslims, which became his *jizya*.[19] If we put these sources aside,[20] the obvious and contextual sense of the verse would rather correspond to the conflicts between Muslims and Jews in Medina. However, whatever the historic circumstance relating to this verse, the problem is that this verse, which belongs to a specific context, has been "universalized" by some Muslims, sometimes in the first part of it, i.e., the appeal to fight, but mainly in the second part, the *jizya*. The latter has been understood as a tax which must be paid by the people of the Book to the Muslim authorities, when the verse in itself indicates that it more likely refers to a kind of spoils of war to be paid by the vanquished to the vanquisher.

And for ideological reasons, some consider this *surah* to be the last *surah* revealed, in order to give it a status as a *surah* of abrogation and in order to assert that, from that time onwards, relations with non-Muslims would be hostile, or those of *dhimmitude,* i.e., the subjection of others as a *dhimmi* community,[21] *dhimmi* being the non-Qur'anic title for the people of the Book.

This period of tension also saw the intensification of the Qur'an's challenge to the Jewish and Christian religions regarding differences in dogma. The central point of divergence between Muslims on the one hand, and Jews and Christians on the other is the person of Jesus. The *surah An-Nisa'* addresses the core of these divergences. In the first place, as is well known, the Qur'an denies the divinity of Jesus, but proclaims him as word and spirit from God: "O people of the Book! Do not go beyond the bounds in your religion; only speak the truth as to God. Certainly, the Messiah, Jesus, son of Mary is the messenger of God, he is His word which He has placed in Mary, and he is a spirit coming from Him. Believe therefore in God and in His messengers" *(An Nisa' 4.171a).*

In the second place, the Qur'an refutes a divine triad: "Do not say: 'Three,' cease from doing so; that will be better for you. God (Allah) is the only God! Glory to Him! How could he have a son? To Him belong that which is in the heavens and upon the earth. God suffices for a protector" *(An Nisa'* 4.171b). This theme is taken up again and addressed directly in a late *surah*: "God said: O Jesus, son of Mary! Is it you who has said to people: 'Take me, and my mother, for two gods apart from God?" *(Al Ma'ida* 5.116). Thus, if the Qur'an does not mention the Trinity, it appears nevertheless, on the basis of these two verses, to refute a form of triad where Jesus and Mary are worshipped as gods and where God (the Father) is relegated to second, or last, place, a similarity to the Meccan religion where the worship of Allat, Uzza, and Manat replaced the worship of Allah.[22] The *surah at-Tawba* follows the same lines, while including the Jews in this theme of attribution of sonship to God which replaces Him both in managing the world, and in worship: "The Jews have said: 'Uzayr is a son of God!' The Christians have said: 'The Messiah is the son of God!' Such is the word that comes forth from their mouths; they copy that which the unbelievers said before them" *(At-Tawba* 9.30). As explained above, the expression "the unbelievers" in Qur'anic terminology refers to the Meccan polytheists. As for Uzayr, here is no consensus on his identity, as he is identified with Ezra by some, and with Isaiah by others.[23]

However, sonship is not the only point of divergence concerning Jesus. The second level of difference concerns Jewish, not Christian, teaching. Circling the Qur'anic verse dealing with the crucifixion are other verses, belonging to a pericope which goes beyond the first level of meaning, i.e., the denial of the crucifixion:

> We have punished them because they have not believed, because they put forward concerning Mary a horrible calumny, and because they have said: "Surely, we have killed the Messiah, Jesus, son of Mary, Messenger of God." Truly they have not killed him, they have not crucified him but it appeared to them that they did so. Those who are in disagreement on this subject remain in doubt; they have no certain knowledge but only follow a conjecture. Surely, they have not killed him but God has raised him up to Himself. God is omnipotent, wise. There is no-one among the people of the Book, who will not believe in him [Jesus] before his death, and he will

be a witness against them on the Day of Resurrection. *(An-Nisa'* 4.156-159)

The last part of this section is truly astonishing, even more so because it is never mentioned in gatherings for interreligious dialogue. The Qur'an not only takes up the defence of Mary and of Jesus, but promises that all the people of the Book – to be understood here as non-Christians, i.e., Jews, Samaritans, Sabians – will believe in Jesus as prophet, Messiah, Word and Spirit of God.

We may also note that the suggestion that Jesus was taken up before his crucifixion and his replacement on the cross by one of his disciples is not mentioned in the Qur'an but is an elaboration of the exegesis of the verse mentioned above ("they have not killed him, they have not crucified him, but it seemed to them that they did so"), as well as of the verse "God then said: 'O Jesus I am going, in truth, to cause you to die *(mutawaffika)*, to raise you up to Myself, to purify you of those who disbelieve, and place those who have followed you above the disbelievers until the Day of Resurrection. Then you will return to Me; I will judge then between you and I will pronounce concerning your differences" *(Al Imran 3.55).*

The commentaries on this verse 3.55 show that the exegetes have been troubled by the expression "*mutawaffika*" (cause you to die) and that they have attempted, particularly from the beginning of the fourth century of the Hijra (tenth century CE) to divert its meaning by providing metaphorical explanations for the term "die." The earliest exegetes, by contrast, do not hasten to deny the death and resurrec-tion of Jesus, particularly because of another verse, where it is Christ himself who speaks: "May Peace be upon me on the day when I was born, on the day when I die, and the day when I will be resurrected" *(Maryam 19.33).* Tabari, for example, cites previous Muslim exegetes who state that Jesus is dead for three hours before being raised up to God.[24] This is referred to in the recent commentary of Ibn Ashour (d. 1393 H/ 1973 CE), who added that Jesus had an exceptional breath of life, more special than that of the other prophets, whose breath of life is in its turn to be distinguished from that of other mortals.[25] The denial of the crucifixion and the resurrection of Jesus, replaced by the idea of a taking up of Jesus and of his return at the end of time, seems therefore to have gradually been introduced into Islamic thought, probably following the polemics between Christians and Muslims and in further response to these polemics.

To return to our chronological outline, apart from the dogmatic and political differences, the Qur'an admonishes, in this third phase of its negotiation with the people of the Book, those among them who are neither faithful to the Balance, nor to commitment to the economy of the Reminder. It denounces, for example, those Jewish scholars and those monks who misappropriate the wealth of their communities: "O you who believe! Know that many scholars and monks devour completely the goods of others and turn people aside from the way of God!" (At Tawba 9.34). At the same time, it emphasizes the unfaithfulness of some toward their own faith, when they alter the meaning of the Scriptures, or turn aside from following Abraham: "There are among the Jews those who remove words from their proper context" (An-Nisa 4.46); and "Why therefore do they envy those whom God has rewarded with His Favour? Surely, We have given to the descendants of Abraham the Book and the Wisdom, and We have given them a vast kingdom. Among them, some have faith in him (Abraham), while others have turned away from him" (An-Nisa' 4.54-55).

However, during the same period and at the heart of these tensions, over and above the three registers of the political, the dogmatic and the call to faithfulness, there is another: a purely theological register. For if, historically and contextually, matters had become complicated and the tension between the different religious groups had exploded, the Qur'an maintains at this point its call at the theological level for all people to realize that salvation is not a question of identity: "This depends neither on your wishes nor those of the people of the Book. Whoever does a bad deed will be punished for that, and will not find in his favour, apart from God, any to support him. And whoever, man or woman, does good works, while being faithful... These are they who will enter Paradise; and no-one will do them harm, no, not even of the size of a date kernel" *(An-Nisa'* 4.123-124). And so at the heart of the tensions, whether political or dogmatic, the Qur'an reminds that the criteria of differentiation in the eyes of God is that of faith and of works, and not of the religious tag worn by men or women.

A New Opening: The Third Period of Revelation

During the final phase of the prophetic mission, the relationship of the Qur'an with the people of the Book would undergo fundamental changes. This was also the phase in which a major transformation took place in the relationship of the Qur'an – and of the first Muslims – with the Meccan polytheists. For this reason, I suggest that, resulting from a thematic and chronological study of the *surah*s, it is worthwhile opening a new section within the traditional chronological division of the Qur'an. Rather than dividing it into two periods, I would suggest a third. Such a new division into three will need to be tested out and verified in later studies. What I propose therefore is that to the Meccan and Medinan periods (including the three phases of the Medinan period outlined above) a third period can be added, particularly represented in the last *surah* that was revealed, *Al Ma'ida*, to which we can find prologues in the *surah*s of the three last years of the revelation.

I consider the *surah Al Hajj* to be among the *surah*s belonging to the end of the prophetic mission, and thus to this third period. It takes up again the question of salvation for the followers of the members of other religions, however less clearly than the *surah al Baqara* (2.62). It is also only in this *surah* that the Zoroastrians (Magians) make an appearance: "Surely, between the believers, the Jews, the Sabians, the Christians, the Magians and the 'associationists,' God will decide on the Day of Resurrection. Certainly, God is witness to everything." *(Al Hajj* 22.17). The ambiguity of this verse has opened the door to multiple interpretations across the centuries, the question being who will be on which side of salvation, the answer varying according to the interpretations. For the most extreme among the exegetes, salvation is only for the Muslims, and God will distinguish them from the others on the Day of Judgment. We may note that this interpretation goes against the text of the Qur'an itself, notably verses 123-124 of the *surah an-Nisa'* mentioned above and which insists on the fact that no one can count on salvation on the basis of their religious identity, also *Al Baqara* 2.62, which promises salvation to the believers and doers of good deeds among the different religious denominations. For some other interpreters, salvation encompasses only the Christians and the Jews, besides the Muslims. A third group of interpreters join the Sabians and the Magians to the Jews and the Christians. Only exceptional Sufis are bold enough to say that salvation may include also the "associationists," by virtue of their *fitra* and of the primordial pact. And the *surah Al Hajj* adds, in confirmation of the wider interpretations of salvation and whom it includes: "For each community, We have established a ritual so that human beings may invoke the name of God over each beast of the herd that he has given them" (*Al Hajj* 22.34).

The principle of religious diversity is also visibly put forward in this period, and it is also extended to the "associationists" of Mecca, who had given Muslims quite a hard time until then. In fact, the relationship between the first Muslims and the Meccan polytheists can also be divided into the three phases. In the Meccan period, the principle of religious diversity was proclaimed in the *surah* entitled "The Disbelievers": "Say: 'O you disbelievers! I do not worship what you worship, and you do not worship what I worship. As for me, I do not worship what you have worshipped any more than you worship what I worship. To you, your religion, and to me my religion!'" (*Al Kafirun* 109.1-6).

This position, however, was overtaken by the whole history of battles and hostility which was to take place during the Medinan period, culminating in a general pronouncement concerning the Meccan polytheists, once again in the problematic *surah, At Tawba*: "The associationists are nothing but impurity" (*At Tawba* 9.28). Nevertheless it is clear that in this third period of the prophetic mission, a new opening has taken place toward those "associationists" who do not fight the Muslims, and we find this in the *surah al Mumtahina,* which reminds Muslims of the example of Abraham and his relationship with his people. The passage deserves to be quoted as a whole, as it shows that the conflict is not a religious one, but one of power and of the preservation of one's self-identity, and that friendship is permitted with those "associationists" who are not among the oppressors:

He has given you a good example in Abraham and in those who were with him, when they said to their people: "We disavow you, you and what you worship apart from God; we renounce you! What is between us and you will not be shown except hostility and hatred until you believe in God, the One!" Nevertheless, Abraham said to his father: "I demand forgiveness for you while I do not have any power except of God." [They prayed,] "Our Lord! We trust ourselves to You! We come back to You! To You will be the return! Our Lord! Do not permit the disbelievers to persecute us, and our Lord, forgive us! Truly You are the Powerful, the Wise." You have in these a good example for those who hope in God and in the last Day. And whoever turns away [should know that] God is the Abundant One, the Worthy of Praise. God will establish perhaps friendship between you and those among them who you consider to be enemies. God is all-powerful, He is the One who forgives, merciful. God does not forbid you to excuse and treat with equity those who have not fought against you because of your faith nor expelled you from your homes. God loves those who are just. God only forbids you to take for friends those who have fought against you because of your faith, those who have expelled you from your homes and those who have worked for your expulsion. Those who take them for their friends, those are the evil-doers! (*Al Mumtahina* 60.4-9)

However, even the condition concerning friendship with the "associationists" – to know that they had not taken part in fighting the Muslims and expelling them from their homes – was to be overtaken by the pardon given by the Prophet to those who had fought against him. When the Muslims returned to Mecca following eight years of exile (that is in year eight of the Hijra), Muhammad entered as conqueror the town he had left as a pariah. The Prophet astonished the Meccans, who awaited a revenge that would encompass them all, by pardoning with his compatriots all those who had fought against him and his community, thus recalling the pardon given by Joseph to his brethren. He reminded them also of the unity and fragility of the human race by referring to the works of God, saying, as reported in a *hadith*: "We are all from Adam, and Adam is of the earth (dust)." Following this, he declaimed the Qur'anic verse: "O people! We have created you of a male and of a female. We have formed you into peoples and tribes so that you might have knowledge one of another. In truth, the most noble among you before God is the one who behaves with piety. God is all-knowing, he is aware of everything" (*Al Hujurat* 49.13).[26]

The message carried by this verse is universal and does not address Muslims alone, nor just people of the Book, for the interpellation 'O people' gives it a universal reference. In fact we see a distinction in the use of interpellation throughout the *surah*s of the Qur'an. During the Meccan period, the interpellation has a universal character: "O people." During the Medinan period, the *surah*s show intensification in the use of an interpellation with a particular reference: "O those who believe," which shows there has been a rift with the others. Then, at the beginning of the *surah Al Hujurat* (therefore at the beginning of the third Qur'anic period), we find the two interpellations side by side, "O people" and "O those who believe," indicating a double reference in the contents of the Qur'an. This usage marks out those verses with a universal reference, speaking to all, from those verses addressed specifically to followers of the new religion.

But we should note that it is in the last *surah* to be revealed,[27] entitled *Al Ma'ida* (the Feast) as if to signify divine hospitality, that the discussion of the subject of the people of the Book, and the address of the Qur'an to them, is taken up again, making room for a kind of recapitulation of the message. For even if this *surah* is at the heart of the period of the new opening, it continues nevertheless in a denunciation of the disrespect for the Balance, and of a carelessness on the part of the religious leaders,[28] and it does not ignore dogmatic differences.[29] All the same, here these differences and reproaches seem to introduce or to be a reminder of theological principles.

The first is that of divine generosity. A verse of this *surah* asserts: "And the Jews say: 'The hand of God is closed!'.... On the contrary, His two hands are wide open: He gives His gifts as he pleases" (*Al Ma'ida* 5.64). The gifts in question here concern spiritual gifts and the connections that God makes with human beings. The sense of the verse is that human beings must not, in the name of the "truth" of their respective religions, ascribe limits to the divine freedom, which certainly goes beyond their understanding.

In other words, God is not the monopoly of anyone and He is at equal distance from the whole world. It is in this way that we can understand the Qur'anic expression, "He is established on the Throne": "Surely Your Lord is God (Allah), who has created the heavens and the earth in six days, next he is established on the throne" (*Al A'raf* 7.54). The root of the term *istawa,* translated by "he is established," signifies both "togetherness" and "at equal distance," and has given its name to the equator (*khatt al istiwa*). For this reason, the *surah al Ma'ida* reproves anyone who claims to possess closeness to the divine to the exclusion of others: "The Jews and the Christians have said: 'We are the children of God, and His chosen ones.' Say: "Why then does he chastise you for your sins?" In fact, you are but human beings among those whom He has created. He pardons those whom He wishes to, and He chastises those whom He wishes. And to God alone belongs the kingdom of the heavens and of the earth and of all which is found between the two. And it is to Him that will be the final arriving" (*Al*

Ma'ida 5.18). This is corroborated by a *hadith* that states: "All creatures are the children of God, and the most close to Him is the one who is the best toward His children."

It is therefore clear that any form of exclusivism or spiritual arrogance is contrary to the message of the Qur'an. Its call is that we may concentrate on faithfulness in religion, love, and good works for the benefit of all. Because of this, the Qur'an calls both Muslims and the people of the Book to follow what has come to them as messages from God, while being clothed in humility: "Say, O people of the Book, you do not hold fast to anything, while you do not conform to the Torah and the Gospel and to that which has been sent down on the part of your Lord" (*Al Ma'ida* 5.68), and "There are surely, among the people of the Book, those who believe in God and in what has been sent down to you and what has been sent down to them. They are humble toward God and never sell His verses and signs at low price. Here are those whose reward is with their Lord" (*Al Imran* 3.199). This humility, shown in Christian priests and monks, provides the criterion whereby a person is considered truly believing: "You will find that the ones most close to the Believers in friendship are those who say 'In truth, we are Christians.' For there are among them some priests and monks, and these are free from arrogance" (*Al Ma'ida* 5.82).

From the fact that Islam belongs to the same economy of the Reminder as the people of the Book, and that Muslims are themselves people of the Book, I consider that the majority of what the Qur'an contains in admonition toward the people of the Book extends also to Muslims. They should not consider themselves sheltered from the divine remonstrance as to their estrangement from the two pacts (covenants), their failure to observe the Balance in their doings, and their quickness to return ill-will toward others, and the arrogance which they have displayed since the first centuries, arrogance described by the Prophet as being a form of hidden "associationism."

Also, in the same times of the prophetic mission, the discovery within the Muslim community of a group of "hypocrites," as mentioned above, has allowed Muslims to see that their community has not been above all suspicion. We can perhaps even see in that discovery the turning point that permitted the "new opening" toward others, even to the "associationists" of Mecca. Iranian philosopher and theologian Abdul Karim Soroush affirms: "Neither the dogma of Muslims nor the dogma of Christians is free from 'associationism.'" The world here below is full of identities which are contaminated, not wholly pure. There is not a clear and pure truth on the one side and a completely clouded falsehood on the other. When we recognize this truth, plurality becomes easier to be accepted."[30]

In this sense, the discovery of the hypocrisy of "associationism" hidden within the first community will have allowed Muslims to make an inner adjustment to their conception of plurality and unity. For if at the beginning of the Medinan period they tried to gather religious diversity into a single religion, at the end of the prophetic mission they are called to see in diversity the sign of a future unity, reconciled in God. For this reason, the Qur'an recalls at this stage the promise of salvation to all believers and doers of good of diverse religions, taking up again almost word for word a verse already cited at the beginning of the Medinan period[31]: "Those who have believed, those who are Jew, Sabians, and the Christians, those who believe in God, and the last day and who accomplish good works, there is no fear for them, and they will not be afflicted" *(Al Ma'ida* 5.69).

This repetition is understood by Mahmoud Ayoub as emphasizing what is most important in the Quranic message with regard to other religions.[32] It is as if the whole relationship with others—above all the people of the Book, and all that it includes of differences and religious quarrels—is incorporated in the setting out of this "doubled" verse, so that at last it is not possible to avoid the message it contains.

Also, the Qur'an introduces at this final stage of the revelation, the hope of a unity through reconciled diversity, upon the return to God,[33] a hope which can be translated here below and made through good works:

We have revealed to you the Book with the Truth, confirming the Scripture which was before him and watching to safeguard it. Judge between these people according to what God has revealed. Do not conform to their desires in turning away from what you have received of the Truth. To each one of you We have given a Law and a Way. If God had wished, He would have made of you one single community, but He has wished to test you through what he has given you. Compete in good deeds. It is to God that you all will return and He will enlighten you on the subject of your differences. *(Al Ma'ida 5.48)*

Thus, following the quarrels, following the perception of the people of the Book as schismatics, comes this last period that sees things as they are: with dogmatic and political divergences, but with communion possible in God and in the works carried out for His glory. And the recognition which is due to others is incontestable, because it is God who affirms that He has willed diversity, just as He affirms that each religious way derives from Him. According to Abdul Karim Soroush, the attitude toward the other religions of the same economy of the Reminder must be an attitude of thanksgiving, for "pluralism does not mean anything at all other than faith in the widenesss of the divine Mercy, to admit the success of the prophets in their prophetic mission, the feebleness of the devil, and the vision of the breadth of the divine Mercy extending to all the corners of the existing world."[34]

And it is to this thanksgiving, and to the celebration of the divine hospitality in which human beings accept their differences, that the final *surah* calls to. The title *Al Ma'ida*, the Feast or the Table, contains the description of a feast sent down from heaven to the disciples of Jesus; but it includes as well another table, this time going heavenwards from earth, a table of communion between believers of different religions that takes them beyond the things that separate them in their daily lives, and yet also goes to the heart of these differences: "Today, things which are good and pure are permitted to you. The food of those to whom the Book has been given is permitted to you, and your food is permitted to them" (*Al Ma'ida* 5.5).

The Muslims with the people of the Book are therefore invited to live together under the shadow of the divine generosity and hospitality, accepting one another, and adorning themselves with generosity and hospitality in the image of their one God.

Islam and the Theology of Other Religions

A careful look at the chronology of the Qur'anic relationship to the religions of the people of the Book and at the relationship of Muslims with the associationists of Mecca, as described in the Qur'an, allows us to infer the pedagogical message of the Qur'an regarding the relation to the other, as well as a Qur'anic theology of other religions.

As we have shown, the Qur'anic relationship to the religions of the Book goes through three phases: an initial appeal based on a religion of Abraham, followed by a phase where the reality of schism and the vicissitudes attending mutual relationships are confronted, and finally at a celebration of fellowship and of communion in works done for God despite the challenge of irreducible difference. It is as if the appeal is for us to see, finally, that there is a *ghayb* (mystery) in the divergence. Human beings are unable to grasp this at the lower level, but through contemplation, looking from where we are in the "here and now" toward the world to come, the challenge can be transformed into a source of grace.

Verse 48 of the *surah al Ma'ida* says: "If God had wished, He would have made of you one community, but He has wished to test you through that which He has given you." The verse continues with the expression "*istabiqu al khayrat.*" This expression can be understood as meaning "excel yourselves in good works," while it can be translated as "anticipate the good things to come." In this sense, the challenge of divergence when accepted as a reality, becomes like a launching platform toward another reality, that of return together toward God; next, the verse continues: "It is to God that all of you will return and

He will enlighten you concerning the object of your differences" *(Al Ma'ida* 5.48).

It is in this expectation, in this orientation toward the return, that believing followers and doers of good from different religions are already united in the here and now, as a prefiguration of their union the hereafter. Does not the Qur'an promise this union of all human beings at the return? "He has created you and he will resurrect you as but one soul" *(Luqman* 31.28).

We should note that this promise embraces all human beings and not just the people of the Book. This is in harmony with the last phase of the Qur'anic relationship with the associationists of Mecca. Similarly to the relationship with the people of the Book, this relationship progresses according to three phases: in the first phase an appeal to join the new faith, in the second a separation which leads to bloody conflicts, and finally, in the third phase, a pardon followed by a divine appeal to renew friendship and to become open in attitude toward all the peoples of the earth, whatever their religious affiliation, so that a mutual knowledge of one another may flourish.

What remains to be said of the categorization of religions? The Qur'an itself only speaks definitively of two categories of religions: Islam in the broader sense, and associationism.

Islam in the broader sense includes, on the one hand, Islam in the restricted sense, Christianity and Judaism, while leaving a margin open for other religions - notably Sabianism and the religion of the Magians referred to in the verses mentioned above;and on the other hand, those personal quests which may not be found tied to one particular religion, but which lead to God and to the just balance.

Regarding those religions which belong to Islam in the broader sense, the Qur'an calls them the religions of the people of the Book *(Ahl al Kitab)* and places the Christians and the Jews at the heart of these religions of the Book. Yet the term "Book" *(Kitab)* is a term of multiple meanings. In Arabic, the same term is used to signify a book, and also a marriage contract. The etymological sense of the root *KTB* signifies to link or join one thing to another.[35] Also, in his work on the different appellations that the Qur'an uses for itself, as the Qur'an names itself "Book," too, Daniel Madigan concludes that the term means a procedure rather than a product, the procedure of a continuous divine engagement with humanity.[36] The Qur'an speaks, in fact, apart from the archetypal primordial pact, of a historic Covenant or of successive covenants belonging to one same revelation, one same Reminder: "When We have concluded the covenant with the Prophets and with you, and with Noah, Abraham, Moses and Jesus, son of Mary, it is a solemn alliance that We have concluded with them in order that God may require an account of the truthfulness of their sincerity" (Al Ahzab 33.7-8). From this, we could infer that the expression Ahl al Kitab also signifies "people of the Covenant," and that Islam sees itself as a continuation of this alliance and as a reminder, and not a replacement, of the previous covenants.

As for associationism, it included the religion of the Meccans and also of the ancient religions of Sumer and of Egypt. It is characterized by inequality, by non-respect of the Balance, and by invented gods that the Qur'an describes as empty names, in other terms names that do not indicate any existing being.

In fact, theologically, the term associationism means two things: to associate other divinities with God, attributing to them power over the world and offering them worship, and to associate one's passions and one's ego with the worship of God. But it is from the linguistic point of view that we can find clarification regarding associationism. The term shirk (association) means "nets," and the verb ashraka, translated as associate, also means to be taken in the nets, that is to say, to suffer a capture by netting.[37] A Qur'anic verse presents an image which picks up the two meanings: "Those who take protectors apart from God are like the spider; it is given a dwelling, yet the dwelling of the spider is the most fragile of dwellings. If only they are able to know!" (Al Ankabout 29.41).

Associationism therefore consists in a religious initiative which complicates the relationship with God. There is the risk of losing the person in the nets of a complex system of belief, not allowing them to climb again up the thread to God, and resulting in a cut of the link with God.

This initiative is the opposite of the Abrahamic initiative which, added to its simplicity, is characterized by a firm grasp of the link with God, described by the Qur'an as a loop or a rope: "You all, hold firmly to the rope of God" (*Al Imran* 3.102); and "He who submits himself before God and who does good seizes the strongest of ropes. It is to God who determines the end of all things" *(Luqman* 31.32). It is for this reason that "God will not pardon whoever associates Him with anything; but, apart from that, He pardons whom He wills" (*An-Nisa'* 4.48).

Considered from the point of view of the divine mercy, this rejection of associationism by God is not to be understood as resulting from an offence against the divine being, but rather from the fact that humans hurt themselves when they cut themselves off from their Creator and his providence.

If in the course of history, some Muslim *ulema* have attempted to consider every religion other than Islam as associationism, in opposition to the Qur'anic definitions, others tend to include the religions of which they have knowledge under the banner of the people of the Book. For even if the people of the Book have been subjected in history to the status of second class citizens among Muslims, their respective religions were nevertheless considered as the best religions following after Islam in an order of hierarchy. In that way, as Farid Esack affirms, "At various times, Hindus, Buddhists, Zoroastrians, Mages and Sabians were included among or excluded from the people of the Book, depending on the theological predilections of the Muslim scholars and, perhaps more important, the geopolitical context in which they lived."[38]

Interestingly enough, the Qadi Abu Yusu Ya'qub (d. 182 H/798 CE), who wrote for Haroun al Rashid the Book of Land Tax (*Kitab al Kharaj*), included, for mercantile reasons, the Sabians, the Magians and the Samaritans in the list of the people of the Book.[39] Shahrastani (d.548H/1153CE), the recorder of heresies, in his book of the religions and sects *(Al Milal wan-Nihal),* invented a category for "those who have the likeness of a book," which included on the one hand the religion of the Magians, among whom he counted Zoroastrians, and on the other hand the dualist religions, among which he counted Manichaeism and Mazdaism. All these religions had for him a status rather similar to the people of the Book or people of the Covenant, from the fact that the first are considered fundamentally monotheist, while the others recognize Abraham.[40] Meanwhile, the scholar of Indian religions, Biruni (d. 440 H/1048CE), attempted to include Hinduism among the religions of the Book, affirming that this religion is fundamentally monotheist and that the learned among its followers affirm their faith in one God with many manifestations.

I think that the uncertainty in which Muslims find themselves with regard to the religions of the world, outside those which clearly belong to Islam in the broader sense or to the economy of the Reminder, is deliberate so far as the Qur'an is concerned. The Book states that God has sent messengers to all the communities upon earth, but He has not necessarily named them in the Qur'an: "There does not exist any community where one who warns has not gone" *(Fatir* 35.24); "[We have also sent a revelation to] some messengers of whom we have spoken to you and some messengers of whom We have not told you the history" *(An Nisa'* 4.164). This suggests that every religion not identified as within the dynamic of associationism may be considered *a priori* as having been founded by a messenger of God, and so is fundamentally part of the economy of the reminder, seeking to remind of the initial witness to divine unity and to the just balance. This is the case, even if with time its initial monotheism has suffered. We need to recollect that even with the followers of better-known religions, notably Judaism, Christianity, and Islam, monotheism and the Balance can suffer distortions in certain contexts.

The question is to know if this applies both to those religions which preceded Islam, and to religions which have come into being subsequently. The refusal to recognize religions subsequent to Islam is based on an interpretation of the expression "seal of the prophets," which appears in the *surah al Ahazb* (33), verse 40: "Muhammad is not the father of anyone among you, but he is the Messenger of God and the seal of the prophets" (*Al Ahzab* 33.40), the term "seal" being explained as the one who sets the seal upon prophecy.

However, this same term can be explained differently and more in conformity with other Qur'anic verses that speak of the relation of Muhammad to the preceding messages. In effect, Muhammad is described as the one who confirms the Torah and the Gospel. In this sense, seal of prophecy may also be understood, as Michel Hayek proposes, as "the one who confirms the prophecy" and not its "sealing up,"[41] which leaves the door open before human beings and before the divine will.

On the other hand, the language of the Qur'an distances itself as much as possible from generalizing concerning identities, introducing such expressions as "certain among them," "a number of," " a faction among," etc. However, it introduces the personal dimension with the verses which promise salvation to Jews, Christians and Sabians: whether in adding to the list every person who believes and does good works (*Al Baqara* 2.62 and al Ma'ida 5.69), or in reminding that salvation is not a question of religious identity but of acts of faith and deeds for the wellbeing of humanity *(An-Nisa' 4.123-124)*.

To this we may add the famous *hadith qudsi,* which, in echo of Matt. 25.34-45, underlines that salvation stems from good deeds toward the other, reflecting the divine in the life of each one:

> God says on the day of judgment, O son of Adam, I was sick and you did not come to see Me, and the man replies, "But you, Lord, when was this so?" And God replies: My servant [*so and so*] was sick and you have not visited him, do you not know that if you had visited, you would have found Me with him? Next God said: I had hunger and you did not feed Me. And the man said: "But how could God have hunger?" And God replied, a certain one had hunger, has asked food from you and you have not given him to eat, do you not know that if you had given him to eat you would have

found that person with Me? O son of Adam, I had thirst and you did not give Me to drink. And the man said: "But how can God have thirst?" And God replied: do you not know that a certain one had thirst, and he asked you to give him to drink and you have not given him to drink? If you had given him to drink you would have found that with Me.

In a linguistic consideration of the terms *iman* (faith) and *kufr* (unbelief) in the Qur'an, Farid Esack shows clearly that these two terms refer to a process which grows and diminishes with each human person throughout their life and their religious and spiritual journey. It is a matter of dynamic, not static, principles in the lives of human beings, even more so as the Qur'an states that these two processes are the result of a double dynamic, where the human being and God are the agent.[42] And Farid Esack concludes that faith and unbelief are not socio-political attributes to ascribe to certain religious communities, but terms which indicate the dynamic of the journey of each person in relation to the divine.[43]

In conclusion, the Qur'an in its pedagogy exhorts Muslims fully to accept and to integrate the principle of diversity as the divine will and as prefiguring a union of reconciliation with divergence which is to come, as we can see from verses such as these: "If your Lord had willed, He would have made human beings of one single community" (*Hud* 11.118), and "To each an orientation toward which he turns himself. Excel in good works and anticipate the good things to come (*istabiqu al khayrat*). Wherever you are, God will gather you to Himself, for God is surely Omnipotent" *(Al Baqara* 2.148).

The Qur'an also invites believing Muslims to accept the limitations on their knowledge, and it seems to encourage them toward a certain agnosticism, not toward the divine, but with regard to other religions. The uncertainty of the Muslim concerning a categorization of the other appears in the Qur'anic teaching as the catalyst of a religious humility and modesty that is required of the believer.

Finally, the Qur'an encourages believing Muslims and doers of good works not to consider others on the basis of their assigned religious identity, but through awareness of their personal relation to the divine and with the Balance. The Qur'an encourages them to cultivate relations with others with a view to getting to know them, seeking to build deeper links across the borders of identity with those in whom they perceive faith and commitment to good works. In this way they will be able to taste together, even in the present times, the "good things which are to come."

5. THE CHURCH AND OTHER RELIGIONS
Toward Spiritual Solidarity

Fadi Daou

Religions: Ways of Salvation?

The Conciliar Declaration on the Church and non-Christian Religions, *Nostra aetate*, affirms that the Catholic Church "rejects nothing of what is true and holy" in religions (*Nostra aetate* 2). When someone approached Jesus with the question, "Good Teacher, what must I do to inherit eternal life?" (Mark 10:17), before replying to his question, Jesus told him, "No one is good but God alone" (Mark 10:18). Elsewhere, Jesus proclaims, according to John's gospel, that he is the Truth (cf. John 14:6). We can therefore conclude that to recognize the existence of the true and of the good in non-Christian religions is to recognize that God is the source of this. Jesus Christ, the eternal Word of God, revelation of his full goodness and truth, is therefore not without connection with other religions.

I would suggest, then, that those who prefer not to admit this kind of recognition of non-Christian religions, and rely for their estimate simply on the appreciation of the experiences and religious actions of individuals, are without solid arguments. They say for example, that *Lumen gentium* 16 recognizes the Abrahamic faith of Muslims and not Islam as such. To make a radical dissociation between the belief experience of the individual and his or her religion represents a lack of discernment and of intellectual and spiritual courage. Furthermore, in his encyclical letter on the mission of Christ the redeemer, John-Paul II entered this discussion, stating clearly that God "does not fail to make himself present in many ways, not only to individuals but also to entire peoples through their spiritual riches, of which their religions are the main and essential expression, even when they contain "gaps, insufficiencies and errors."[1]

The Authenticity of the Faith of Other Believers

The declaration of the Congregation for the Doctrine of the Faith, *Dominus Iesus*, affirms that "the various religious traditions contain and offer religious elements which come from God, and which are part of what 'the Spirit brings about in human hearts and in the history of peoples, in cultures, and religions.'"[2] The same document distinguishes, however, between "theological faith" and belief. Thus, according to the text, while faith is reserved to Christians who accept the truth revealed by God the Three in One, belief expresses the range of experiences and of reflections which the human beings develop, in their quest for truth and for relationship with the divine.

This distinction is not free from ambiguity, particularly when it is read in the light of the affirmation which precedes it concerning the presence of God in other religions. It reveals hesitations which remain persistent within certain circles in the Catholic magisterium, with regard to the Christian theology of religions. It is necessary to say that the revolution which Christianity, and notably the Catholic Church, has experienced in this area is "Copernican." It is sometimes sensible to look back in order not to forget where one has come from, and to give thanks for the way ahead. But this looking behind must not become the expression of a nostalgia or of a doubt concerning the work that God has accomplished through God's people, after the example of Lot's wife who became a column of salt because she was not able to resist seeing Sodom in flames, from whence God had rescued her (cf. Gen.10:26).

To return to the distinction between the theological faith of Christians and the belief of others, I would like to make three comments. First of all, to me it does not seem correct to make a separation between faith, a gift of God, and belief, the attitude of human beings toward God. Even for the Christian religion, faith and belief represent two faces of a single reality. God certainly gives the grace of faith in himself with the help of the Holy Spirit, aiding human beings in their response to the divine initiative. But what would a faith be without any response on the part of human beings? Isn't the Christian faith alive to the extent to which believers receive it in their lives and it becomes a source of inspiration for all their practices and daily activities? To separate in this way between faith and belief is to make an artificial and inappropriate division between the work of God in the life of human beings and the response of believers to God's calling. God acts in the very being of the human person and through our personal journeys. Faith is therefore truly a gift of God; but it is the gift of a relationship, not simply the gift of an intellectual truth or experience that is external to the person. So in this relationship of love and trust, God offers the grace of faith to people who live out this grace in their belief and their daily life, in faithfulness and in thanksgiving.

My second remark is regarding the sense of recognition of a presence of God in other religions. When the document *Dominus Iesus* confirms that the elements of religious life to be found in non-Christian religions may come from God, it seems difficult to me after that recognition to deny this divine providence with regard to the most sublime and profound act of religious expression, namely the personal relationship which a human being seeks to build with God. Speaking of the prayer of non-Christians, John Paul ll affirms that "all authentic prayer is sustained by the Holy Spirit who is mysteriously present in the heart of each person."[3] If God is not then a stranger to the spiritual experiences of non-Christian believers, the faith they profess becomes in this sense a place of the manifestation of divine grace, and an expression of the covenant of love which joins them to him.

Finally, the third comment leads me to recall the encounters of Jesus with those foreign to his Jewish religion, referred to above. When Christ expressed his admiration for the faith of the centurion or the Canaanite woman, he was recognizing at the same time the work of the Father in their lives, and the spiritual experience and trust in God that flourished in their hearts.

As a result, to move beyond this superficially dualist view of the relationship between faith and belief, we must recognize, with Mgr Joseph Doré, the following principle: if Christ works out the salvation of non-Christians through being present and acting in the religions to which they belong, he does this through the intervention of his Holy Spirit. The Holy Spirit comes in this way to bring to fulfilment the life which has already come to fruition among the faithful of those religions through the action of the same Spirit, active through the means which they themselves have offered.[4]

While maintaining that Christ is the sole mediator between God and humanity, and that he is at the centre of all authentic spiritual experience, the Christian may also recognize that his mediation can take place through three kinds of intermediary: the Holy Spirit, the church, and the specific means of grace and holiness in other religions. Vatican ll affirms that "as the one goodness of God is radiated in different ways among his creatures, so also the unique mediation of the Redeemer does not exclude but rather gives rise to a manifold cooperation which is but a sharing in one source" (*Lumen gentium* 62).

Incorporated in the unique mediation of Christ, the religions may therefore play their role by participating in mediation between believers and God. Recognizing the work of God and of his grace in the belief experience of non-Christians allows me, therefore, to affirm the theological value and authenticity of their faith, in the measure to which this faith is sincere and coherent with God's design of love and salvation.

Other Religions: A Positive Challenge for the Church

We can say that the encounter of the church with each religion constitutes a positive challenge for Christian theology. When taking place in dialogue, and according to the proper rules of the theological disciplines, this encounter may lead to a deepening in the Christian understanding of the mystery of salvation, of the presence of Christ, and of the action of the Spirit through the plurality of the religions and spiritual journeyings. John Paul ll therefore believed that other religions encourage the church to discover and recognize the signs of the presence of Christ and the action of the Spirit in the world, helping it as a result to deepen its own identity (cf. *Redemptoris missio,* 56.)

We can also mention for example, the appreciation, even admiration, Christians express for the experiences of the Sufis in the Muslim world. They see in these mystics the expression of an experience of divine love and of the closeness of God to humanity, even of union with him. Sometimes one can identify there a Christlike dimension, without it being openly named as such. Muslims do not hesitate for their part to praise the virtues of certain Christian religious, and to admire their permanent consecration to the adoration of God in the most radical detachment and humility.

To know how to appreciate and recognize the spiritual experiences of others is a religious virtue. However, often this appreciation remains at the level of attraction to what is in common between the different religions. Or rather, one appreciates in the other faith the things which recall the message of one's own religion. So, when Christians express a positive view of Sufi Muslims, it is because their experience reveals something of the universal mystery of Christ. In the same way, when the Muslims admire the monastic life, it is because it shows an attachment above all to the one God, preached by the Qur'an.

Certainly, for some Christians even this kind of recognition is somewhat difficult. Those who are in fear of others or mistrust them are actually incapable of seeing the work of God outside their own religious space. They prefer rather to express and transmit stereotypes and prejudiced descriptions of the religion of the other. Among Christians, those conversations, emails, or even books are not uncommon that implicitly seek to denigrate the faith of Muslims. To do this gives the impression of being in harmony with the current of the times! It is this that makes the task of those who are determined instead to live in the breath of the Spirit more difficult and more urgent.

Of these last, having their eyes open to the immensity of the work of God and of his mercy, it is required to go further in this experience of mutual recognition. The real challenge is met by openness to the mystery of the divine in its diversity, even if this is disconcerting, and by the ability to appreciate the spiritual riches of the other, in their particularity, and in their difference compared to our own. All the same, it is necessary to say that one cannot demand this of everyone. Such an attitude of openness demands a great maturity in one's own faith, and a real experience and knowledge of the other, and of that "other religion" which is encountered.

To accept others, in their religious otherness and the richness of their spiritual experience, seems to me a prerequisite for developing a Christian theology of other religions. It is this openness to the particularity of the experience of other believers which permits Christians, in the light of faith in Jesus Christ, to venture more deeply into depths of God's plan of salvation. It is as if, in this particular realm, the other becomes a key of interpretation for our faith. The Catholic patriarchs of the Orient express this strongly by saying "the presence of others is the voice of God in our life."[5]

To give to the other this role in our own theological development and belief allows the theology of religions to avoid two pitfalls. On the one hand, believers of other faiths, when viewed through the richness of their spiritual experience, encourage us not to avoid the difficult theological conversation concerning the recognition – or not

– of the "divine status" of other religions. The efforts of Christian theologians of religions are surely praiseworthy and indispensable in addressing interpretations of the divine plan of salvation and the problems regarding the unity and unicity of divine revelation when faced with religious pluralism. We must not forget, however, that the divine plan is a mystery, whose knowledge depends on the divine will, which reveals it to those who are capable of understanding its meaning, not just at the intellectual theological level, but in terms of the lived experience of communion with God. The study of the religious experience and spirituality of the other is, therefore, a work which is at one and the same time theological and spiritual.

On the other hand, those of other religions that accompany us in our theological reflections on their experience and on the gifts with which God provides them prevent us from falling into essentialism, that is, into a pre-judgment regarding the necessary attributes of a particular religion. In actual fact, in the interior of each religion there is a great diversity of experiences and interpretations. As a result, I think that a Christian theology of religions can only be shaped where it is possible to include theological reflection developed through contact with a particular religion and with its own cultural context. Religious "otherness" is, therefore, impossible to consider theologically in the absence of the other, so as not to reduce this other to a monolithic and fixed identity. This saves us from the temptation and the naivety of a dualist vision that only allows for two opposing camps: ourselves and others.

Religious otherness is therefore a challenge not only because of its irreducible difference and its insoluble character, hence impossible to incorporate in an artificial unity, but also because of the complexity and internal diversity of each religion. The inexhaustible mystery of salvation and the work of God in the world are manifested equally through the multiplicity of spiritual journeys to the interior of each religious tradition. To choose the authentic way of religious dialogue and to want to enter into the knowledge of another religion means, therefore, taking up the challenge of struggling without ceasing along a pathway marked out by the nature of the walk undertaken, and subject to the encounters and relationships formed en route.

The Relativity of Religions and the Absoluteness of God

Over the course of the last three decades, the Catholic Church has not ceased to denounce relativism as being one of the major perils of the faith.[6] Apart from the fact that it can signal a resignation from seeking the truth which we cannot entertain, it can be defined more positively. According to Cardinal Joseph Ratzinger, who became Pope Benedict XVI, it can be defined positively as "having recourse to the ideals of tolerance, of knowledge gained through dialogue and of liberty, the application of which has been limited by the conception of a truth of universal value."[7] As a result, a system of liberty in thought should be, by its nature, a system of relative positions which are mutually recognized, communicating between one another and remaining open to new developments, without which they cannot be reduced to a common truth. While this is legitimate in the field of politics, this concept becomes dangerous, according to Ratzinger, when it is adopted in the field of religion and of ethics, and more particularly in the domain of the theology of religions.[8] This latter application, defined as "a pluralist theology of religions," at all times represents for the Cardinal a typical product of the encounter between Western post-metaphysical rationalism and the metaphysical religious relativism of the Asiatic traditions.

Thus, a theology of religions which shares in an *a priori* ideology of relativist pluralism, and which puts in question therefore the uniqueness of the mediation in Jesus Christ, cannot remain faithful to Christian tradition. Similar positions can be legitimately understood as the product of the dominant culture during a particular epoch. On the other hand, we must not confound this excess with the theology of religions itself which, following on from Vatican II, in the case of

Catholicism, has developed both as a fruit and as a grace of the opening of the church toward the cultures and religions of the world.

I would critique relativism, but at the same time I distrust a Eurocentrist theology which interprets Christian truths in the light of an exclusively Greco-Latin *logos,* incapable of faithfully apprehending the totality of the spiritual and religious experiences of humanity. In fact, I believe that the labour pains which have come upon the theology of religions, the theology of inculturation, or upon political theology reveal a paradigmatic change in the formation of fundamental theology, which introduces us to a broader conception of the *logos,* both in terms of symbol and of narrative. Oriental Christian theology can rely upon its Antiochean and patristic patrimony in order to assist at this birth. I hope to be able to return to the crucial question very soon in another piece of work.

To refute relativism does not hinder me, however, from speaking of the relativity of each religion before the mystery of God, always much greater! For if one thinks that each religion is a universal system enclosed on itself and which, in addition, believes that it has a monopoly of absolute truth and an exclusive ability to offer salvation to human beings, one arrives both easily and logically at the impossibility of any mutual recognition between religions, and so on to "the war of the gods, without end."

In order to succeed in any interreligious relationship, it is necessary first of all that each should be clear in themselves on a number of points. First, each religion, and more particularly Christianity and Islam, has to recognize explicitly and mindfully in daily practice and in the development of its theological and pastoral discourse that it is not its own reference. It has to remember that its existence and its mission find their meaning in God and his universal plan for the whole of humanity and the totality of creation. Religion is not an end in itself. The church recognizes that its *raison d'etre* is to be in the service of the unity of human beings and their communion with God.

Second, a religion must refuse the temptation, so close to all ideological systems, to claim to have the monopoly of the truth. For God alone is absolute truth. Religions are in the service of this truth, so that human beings may come to accept it, approach it, understand it, interpret it, but never seize upon it, still less manipulate it. Religion is, in fact, in the hands of human beings, all of us creatures of frailty and sinners. Regarding Christians being called into question by others, the Vatican document *Dialogue and Proclamation* warns us that "notwithstanding the fullness of God's revelation in Jesus Christ, the way in which Christians sometimes understand their religion and practice it may be in need of purification" (*Dialogue and Proclamation* 32). Vatican ll reminds us also that "as the centuries go by, the Church is always advancing toward the plenitude of divine truth" (*Dei Verbum* 8). The truth, therefore, is more of a horizon which the church and the believer are summoned toward, than a private property at the disposal of those to whom it belongs.

Third and finally, every religion needs to define itself in terms of journeying and not as a static reality, lest it fall into idolatry. The manner in which some believers think and practice their religion shows that their fundamental attachment is oriented toward a particular practice, a particular text, dogma, guide, or spiritual leader, rather than toward God. There are some religious attitudes which are in reality idolatries, or adoration of human persons, which sometimes hide behind slogans pretending to defend the purity of the faith.

To sum up, we are invited to begin by recognizing our own limitations, and to cultivate humility toward God, his goodness, his wisdom, and his mercy, so that we may practise openness and hospitality toward the members of other religions in a sincere and authentic dialogue. "If only" – suggests Paolo Dall'Oglio – "we were to admire the enormous work of God in every soul, in every tradition, in every human family, then our soul would enlarge, our heart open, our eyes shed forth tears, and our intelligence would be caught up in a vertigo of amazement at the presence of truth!"[9]

In fact the positive recognition of other religions has been achieved in the degree to which the church has been able to resist claiming mastery over the fate of human beings. Yet we should always affirm, together with this recognition, that it is in Jesus Christ that human beings are called to find fullness of life. We therefore find ourselves faced with the great paradox of the need for authentic recognition of "the other," and the duty of mission. To take up this paradox, despite its hard and difficult character, is for me far more truthful and honest than to fall into a complacent relativism on the one hand, or into a diminishment of divine liberty on the other.

To Betray the Mission?

The missionary dynamic: between crisis and renewal

Despite coming to awareness regarding the divine work outside its visible frontiers, the church has not abandoned its role of evangelization. Pope Paul VI reminded us that "The presentation of the Gospel message is not for the church an optional endeavour; it is the duty which is placed upon it."[10] This conviction reminds us of the words of the apostle Paul, who said: "If I proclaim the Gospel, this gives me no grounds for boasting, for an obligation is laid on me, and woe betide me if I do not proclaim the Gospel!" (1 Cor. 9:16). The words of Paul mean, however, that the mission is not an external obligation placed upon him but an interior calling, by reason of the love of Christ which fills his life, without being possible to contain.

In the homily which inaugurated his pontificate, Pope Benedict XVI reminded the world that "the Church as a whole and all her pastors, like Christ, must set out to lead people out of the desert, toward the place of life, toward friendship with the Son of God, toward the One who gives us life, and life in abundance."[11] It is clear then that the openness of the church toward other religions and to the divine presence in them does not lead to any abandonment of a special understanding of its identity and of its specific role in the universal plan of salvation.

By its nature, the church is missionary, and its mission is imperative (cf. *Ad gentes* 2). This is the necessary conclusion from the fact that the church considers itself the depository of the fullness of divine revelation, and to be the sacrament of the kingdom of God in the world.

Christ has called his disciples to be the salt of the earth and the light of the world (cf. Matt. 5:13-14). Their presence is therefore to be directed toward the service of others, and it brings an important dimension to the world, as the salt is for nourishment and the light for life. Pope Benedict XVI stated that proclamation and the witness to the gospel is the first service that Christians must give to each person and to the human race in general.[12]

Yet it is not difficult to observe that the missionary dynamic, particularly so far as the Catholic church is concerned, is in our days much weakened, or at least it has been transformed in a disconcerting way. Already in his encyclical on the mission of Christ the Redeemer, John-Paul ll expressed his unease with regard to a tendency toward the weakening of missionary activity, notably *ad gentes*, that is, toward non-Christians (cf. *Redemptoris missio* 2). More recently, the Congregation for the Doctrine of the Faith has published a doctrinal note on certain aspects of evangelization[13] that seeks to confront a growing confusion leading many people to leave to one side the missionary commandment of Christ. This text appears to wish to recall Catholics to a clearer and more precise conception of missionary engagement, for it affirms strongly that they are called to give priority to the conversion of others to Christ and to the Catholic faith.[14] And the doctrinal note affirms that the goal of mission is the extension of the Catholic Church.[15]

However, as a result of a fear of change in the attitude and outlook of Christians concerning mission, we may lose sight of the actual issues, and risk undermining the meaning of mission itself. For Christian mission only finds its meaning when it is seen as belonging to the universal plan of salvation, where God, by his Word and his Spirit, is the principal "missionary." And so the objective of mission cannot be different from that of God, namely, the salvation of all humanity and of all creation by the bringing about of his kingdom of love, justice, and peace. Consequently, the church is the servant of mission and not its final goal, just as God is the final destination for the believer – not the church, being itself the vessel that guides or aids others in their crossing.

Thus, mission collaborates in the transfiguration both of humanity and of the cosmos, and does not halt just at the promotion of a purely intellectual truth. That is why I believe that the crisis for mission is less the weakening of missionary engagement than the difficulty of grasping the current transition in the concept, and in missionary practice. I see this change positively, because it recalls Christians to an awareness of the richness and complexity of mission. The document *Dialogue and Proclamation* reminds us of the constituent elements of mission: "presence and witness, commitment in social development and human liberation, liturgical life, contemplative prayer, interreligious dialogue and finally proclamation and catechesis" (*Dialogue and Proclamation* 2).

Dialogue versus proclamation?

Looking at the complexity of mission and its relationship with the divine plan in this way, it becomes difficult to think of mission according to the classic terminology of "fishing," or of grand appeals for conversion to "the true faith." But all the same, there are still elements of contradiction and of mistaken witness in some missionary institutions which turn the faith into a product that one seeks to promote and to sell according to marketing methods. Christian Salenson acutely observes that our missionary schemas are polluted by the ideology of our times. For he reminds us that "mission is not born of a surplus that we are obliged to communicate to others, it is born of a *lack of the other* without whom, and in lack of any encounter, I may never liberate my Magnificat."[16]

We need some time in order to liberate ourselves from a notion of mission – and for some a nostalgia – that takes the view that colonialism, Western civilization, and Christian mission were only several facets of the same reality over the course of the centuries: that of the march of humanity toward its earthly and heavenly salvation. Here is not the place to embark upon the history of mission, and we must certainly recognize the heroism and great works of faith and humanity of many missionaries. But it is also necessary to realize that a fundamental mutation has come about in the church's understanding of its missionary nature. It is not, however, a matter of "de-missionizing" mission but of courageously drawing theological conclusions from this new clarity, a clarity which results from the church's renewed awareness of the extent of God's work outside its visible limits. New avenues are now already being explored, such as the concepts of inculturation and the evangelization of cultures. And we must not forget the cosmic dimension of mission, which begins with the evangelization of the relationships that Christian have with others and with the whole of creation.

Thus interreligious dialogue, which has its own value in itself, is equally related to mission in the larger sense. Mission then becomes quite different from a strategy that conceals an attitude favouring proselytism. It is, instead, the result of the profound respect which the Christian must have toward all that the Spirit, who "breathes where he wills," works in human beings. Also, Christians engaged in dialogue do not put their faith in parentheses. Rather, it is in giving account of the hope that is in them (cf. 1 Pet. 3:15) that they give meaning to dialogue, which then becomes an authentic sharing of spiritual riches. "In this way, the partners in dialogue proceed in response to the divine call of which they are conscious. All, both Christians and the followers of other religious traditions, are invited by God himself to enter into the mystery of his patience, as human beings seek his light and truth" (*Dialogue and Proclamation* 84).

Is there a contradiction between respect for religious otherness, dialogue, openness to the work of God in other religions, and mission? Can mission be replaced by these other quantities? There is no simple answer to these questions. Two Roman institutions, the Pontifical council for interreligious dialogue and the Congregation for the evangelization of peoples, brought together their efforts in 1991 with the publication of a consultation document on the subject, entitled

Dialogue and Proclamation. This text has kept its relevance and importance, above all because it makes explicit important positions upheld by Pope John Paul ll in his encyclical *Redemptoris Missio,* referred to above.

The document declares without hesitation that interreligious dialogue is truly part of the dialogue of salvation in which God engages with all humanity (cf. *Dialogue and Proclamation* 80). In this dialogue perspective, the church finds itself in reciprocal relationship with other religions. By its witness to the values of the gospel, the church questions these religions. And to the extent that it is itself marked by human limitations, the church may be questioned by other religions.

Thus, the members of the church and of other religions "find themselves to be companions on the common path which humanity is called to tread" (*Dialogue and Proclamation* 79). John Paul ll, at the closure of the Interreligious Day at Assisi, had already spoken of this way of companionship in which we accompany one another toward a transcendent goal which God prepares for all.[17] And so the church engages in interreligious dialogue, convinced that it is a theological obligation. It is the means of collaborating with the plan of God, by his own methods of presence and of love for all human beings (cf. *Dialogue and Proclamation* 39).

Above all, the mission that Christ entrusts to his apostles is a mission of witness and teaching. So far as conversion is concerned, it is demanded of believers themselves. In fact the Bible never says, "Convert them!" while there are many appeals such as, "Be converted yourselves!" The work of conversion takes place uniquely in the hiddenness of the relationship which links each person to God. It is never completed because one is not converted to a religion but to God in person, in the context of an experience which is both religious and spiritual.

In view of this, I firmly believe that one cannot imprison people in a religious affiliation with a concept of fixed faith identity. Respect for liberty of conscience and the possibility for each person to change their religion is not just a requirement of modern culture. It represents a necessity for faith and for its continued growth and development.

For without liberty, it is impossible to have a covenant, and therefore an authentic relationship with God.

Beyond recognition: spiritual solidarity

There is a great difference between two approaches to the issue of religious otherness. One way is to set out from the nature of one's own religion and its universal mission. The other approach is to change the "point of departure," making this the nature of God and his universal love and mercy toward the whole of humanity. Theologically speaking, the two approaches are not contradictory but complementary. From the Christian point of view, this represents the complementarity which exists between faith in God the Creator and Providence on the one hand, and Jesus Christ the Redeemer on the other. However, it is true that the two approaches give rise to divergent responses concerning religious otherness, because their theological concerns are different, and the questions they are addressing are not the same.

In the case of Christianity, to begin from the church and the particularity of the Christian faith leads toward discussion of the specific nature of Christian identity and of Christian mission toward others. In contrast, to begin from the universal mystery of salvation which God himself carries out through his covenants with humanity and the recapitulation of creation in Jesus Christ allows the Christian to perceive the work of God in the life of other believers and in their religions. And this is without losing sight of the originality of the Christian faith and of its particular role in God's universal design.

It is the second approach which I have adopted throughout this reflection. This approach leads us to that place of divine encounter where all the spiritual history of humanity finds its meaning in the light of the universal and unchanging love of God. Thus we find the following exhortation in the document *On Christianity and the Religions*: "The Christian today must learn to live with respect for religious diversity, in a form of communion which has its foundation in the love of God for humanity and which is based upon his respect for human freedom."[18] Speaking of interreligious dialogue, the same document recalls the presence of God as follows: "Whether these dialogues are the work of specialists or take place in daily life by means of words and behaviour, they are not only an engagement on the part of the human persons who dialogue, but also, and first of all, on the part of the God in whom they believe. Interreligious dialogue, such as it is, includes three partners."[19]

Partners in this dialogue are therefore not only meeting before God but they are also together with God, or rather God with them. This reminds us of the words of Christ to his disciples: "Where two or three are gathered together in my name, there I am in the midst of them" (Matt. 18:20). In a conference on "The necessity of interreligious dialogue in the modern world," the Ecumenical Patriarch of Constantinople Bartholomew I affirms that when "the spirit and the heart open themselves to the possibility of dialogue, something holy takes place."[20]

The Dialogue Intermonastique (DIM),[21] which brings together Christian men and women in religious orders with those of similar dedication in other religions, notably Buddhist, constitutes a strong symbol of this communal spiritual disposition before God. At the origin of this initiative we find two great pioneers of spiritual interreligious dialogue, Henri Le Saux and Thomas Merton.

Interreligious dialogue, according to the website of DIM, widens the practice of monastic hospitality. This takes place in receiving the guest, or by being received in turn, in sharing together a life in fellowship of prayer and work, but still more profoundly by accepting another religious way, by welcoming and entering into an encounter which deepens the Christian way of being present within the plan of salvation. Yusho Sasaki, a Zen Japanese sister, sums up her experience of monastic life shared with the Benedictine sisters of the Abbey of Martigné-Briand (France), by saying: "From both sides, what we are seeking is the same thing. One seeks God, and it is necessary to seek that which transcends language."[22]

Our reader will have already understood this. The theology put forward in this book is not purely theoretical. Some will think that this weakens its impact. For me it is exactly the opposite. As Paolo Dal'Oglio has said so well: "Without the fragrance of witness, all words have the same weight and the same scent. Unless this takes hold of our senses, the truth remains colourless and insipid"[23] Thus, I have wanted to show the effect of a vision of the other illuminated by faith in God, by his infinite and merciful love and inexhaustible wisdom, yet also his closeness to humanity by the gift of himself for all. The way thus traced leads to the recognition of the other, and to the recognition of God in the other, and beyond recognition, to spiritual solidarity.

For the Oriental Catholic Patriarchs, "spiritual solidarity" between Christians and Muslims is in the first place

> a common prayer before God, for oneself and for the other. Before God we are not able to be alone. Before him we bring the feelings and hopes of our brothers, different from us, as we bring our own feelings and our own hopes. We pray to him for them as for ourselves. For if we wish to bring ourselves before the presence of the divine, God wishes that we present ourselves before Him with all our brothers, those who believe like us, and those who believe differently.[24]

In their clarity, these words constitute a message which is both original and audacious, above all because it comes from a church which has accompanied Islam since its origins and knows the joy as well as the pains of this relationship. Spiritual solidarity is here presented, not as an exceptional experience of a "mystical elite" but something which is a divine requirement for every believer. In this way, the authenticity of the spiritual experience can be seen as a tributary of the largesse of spirit and of heart of the one who lives it. It is a requirement of spiritual hospitality where the other finds their being in the interior space of the relationship of the believer with God. In fact the patriarchs insist that our relations with others form an essential part of our spiritual identity.

Christian de Clergé speaks similarly of a possible communion between believers of different religions, with Christians and Muslims in mind. This communion may even be expressed in actuality, in prayer together as a polyphonic celebration of the wonders of the One. He writes:

Let us not doubt the ability to respond to an appeal to prayer encompassing all the ways of spiritual emulation in order join them together better in the gift of God. We may then taste an authentic communion in the differences which are combined, a polyphonic celebration of the innumerable wonders and mercies where the One has imparted his inimitable signs across all our resemblances. A moment of pure joy where, in the harmony of hearts is expressed the desire to share with whoever comes, a prelude to the day of the great gathering together where God will be "all in all." (1 Cor. 15:28)[25]

6. Recognition and Communion

Nayla Tabbara

Islam between Message and Witness

From universal claims to universality

"Anyone familiar with the history of Christianity and Islam sees that the universality of love and of compassion, as it appears in the Gospel and in the Qur'an, is quickly transformed into a limitation of this love and this compassion to a specific dogma [i.e. religious confession], excluding all those who do not accept this dogma," states Mahmoud Ayoub.[1]

In fact, in Islam a theory quickly makes its appearance that denies verses 2.62 and 5.69, which promise salvation to believers and the righteous among Jews, Christians, Sabians, and others, and asserts that with the arrival of Islam these religions have been abrogated by Islam in the narrower sense. However, this theory, which states that Islam, while recognizing the divine origin of the religions of the Book and their spirituality, nevertheless abrogates their laws by Islamic law, is not accepted unanimously and never has been. The exegete Tabari opposes it, affirming that God has promised salvation to all those who are mentioned in *surah* 2.2, and that he has not revoked this promise with the coming of the Islamic revelation.[2] The great Ash'arite theologian Razi (d. 606 AH / 1209 CE) also sees in this exclusivist theory a denigration of the messages of all the prophets,[3] which contradicts the principles of the Islamic faith. Abdelmajid Charfi also states that the Qur'an does not mention at any point the abrogation of the messages of Moses and of Jesus.[4]

Two matters have troubled Muslim exegetes and theologians, driving them to opt for this theory of abrogation of the former messages. On the one hand is the confusion which they have been unable to resolve between Islam in the broader sense (*hanifiyya*) and Islam in the narrower sense. On the other hand are the verses which promote the universality of the Muslim message and of the role of Muhammad: "We have indeed sent you to the whole of humanity as the announcer of the good news, and as warner; but the majority of people do not recognize this" (*Saba'* 34.28); "Say: 'O human beings! I am, in truth, the Messenger toward you all from God to whom belongs the Kingdom of the heavens and of the earth'" (*Al A'raf* 7.158).

How therefore can this universality be reconciled with the diversity willed by God and affirmed in the Qur'an (*Al Ma'ida* 5.48; *Al Baqara* 2.148)? The Qur'an itself replies in the *surah Al Anbiya'*: "We have not sent you but as a mercy for the worlds. Say: 'It has been revealed to me only that your God is One God. [To him] are you submitted?'" (*Al Anbiya'* 21.107-108). The universality of the role of Muhammad resides, therefore, in the fact that he brings a reminder of the Oneness of God, to which all human beings were originally witnesses. In this sense, his message must find an echo with all those who belong to the economy of the Reminder, helping them to recover their true faith if they are estranged from it, and to proclaim the principles of the religions of the Reminder to those who have not been party to this: "Proclaim the Reminder! For there is nothing required of you but to proclaim the Reminder" (*Al Ghashiya* 88.21). The universality of the message is not, therefore, a pretension to universal dominance or a tendency to monopolize religion. This universality resides in the fact that the message regards itself as a universal reminder, belonging to the economy of the Reminder, not seeking to increase the number of followers of a particular religion, but to remind human beings of the foundation of all things: God.

In this sense, the great mystic Hallaj (d. 309 AH / 922CE) is not so far from the meaning of the Qur'an and the intended import of its message when he proclaims:

> I have reflected on the religions and applied myself to understand them, and I have found that they are like the one tree trunk with numerous branchings out. Do not demand of anyone therefore to adopt a particular religion, for it will divert them from the solid and unique trunk. It is the Principle Himself who seeks human beings, and it is in Him that they will find the fulfilment of all aspirations and all meanings. Then they will understand them.[5]

Tunisian Islamic scholar Hmida Ennaifer comes to the same conclusion that the universality of Muhammad's message should not be transformed into an exclusive dogma either at the religious or cultural level. According to him, Muhammad's message recalls the messages of the three prophets who, in the Qur'an, represent universality: Adam, Noah, and Abraham. He sees Abraham in the Qur'an as the founder of the *hanifiyya*, a way that transcends those closed identities which exclude others from divine providence. Noah also represents *hanifiyya* in the Qur'an as being religion in its original conception *(fitra)*, and so refutes the exclusion of human communities from divine mercy. Ennaifer also refers to the story of Adam in its three most relevant aspects: his creation out of the soil of the earth, his life in Paradise followed by his fall, and finally his vicegerency *(khilafa)*, which will become the *khilafa* of his descendents. According to Ennaifer, this allowed a new concept to be introduced to the tribes to which the Qur'an was first addressed: the idea of the universal human, which has existed since ancient times and which is found across the world.

This concept is then employed to transcend the Arab tribal mentality, where the concept of being human is limited to the horizon of the god of the tribe and the ancestor, whose individuality is crushed by the yoke of the tyranny of tribalism. The use that the Qur'an makes of these three persons, Adam, Noah, and Abraham, as proof of universality allows the building of a universal vision, and that in a region which is culturally isolated compared to the unicity of the world as a whole. "The Qur'anic *hanifiyya* shows, by means of the characteristics of the three founding figures, a unicity from a global perspective which is freed from the limits of an oppressive confessionalism, a unicity which both accepts the historic 'givens' and interacts with them." He adds: "This concept established by these three figures," he adds, "encourages us to think of cultural plurality as being an inherent part of the history of unicity, which does not seek to abolish this plurality but can only be realized by means of it and through the enlargement of its horizon."[6]

This is exactly the opposite of the way the message was explained at the time of the conquests, where the universality of the message was "tribalized," making out that it is an exclusivist Islam with universal pretensions that is to be exported to the nations: that is, instead of a reminder of universal significance addressed to the *fitra* of every human being and respecting cultural differences and differences of religious practice. The Grand Imam of Al Azhar, Ahmad at-Tayyib, also deplores that fact that in our days it is tribal thinking that is spreading abroad in the Islamic world.[7]

The nature of witness

If then religious and cultural pluralism are willed by God, and if the role of the prophet is uniquely that of bringing the Reminder, what remains for mission (*da'wa*)? Here also the Qur'an makes its response, transforming our vision of things: "Who therefore pronounces more beautiful words than the one who calls on God, acts virtuously and proclaims: 'Surely I am one of those who submit themselves'?" (*Fussilat* 41.33).

According to this verse, Muslims are not called to convert others to Islam in the narrower sense but to call upon God. They have the duty of being witnesses of God and of serving the reminder to others by their submission to God, by their faithfulness, their piety and their respect for the archetypal pacts that were concluded with God. They are called to be examples, as Abraham is an example for them: "He has given you a good example in Abraham" (*Al Mumtahina* 60.4). At the same time they are called to be witnesses, just as Muhammad has been a witness for them: "Thus We have made of you a mediating community in order that you should witness to humanity, and so that the Prophet should be a witness to you" (*Al Baqara* 2.143).

Muhammad witnessed before his community about the relationship it is possible to have with God and of nearness to him, just as Abraham, who was the friend of God.[8] In their turn, Muslims are called to witness that one can have this personal connection, an intimate one, with God. In other words, they are to remind others of the primordial covenant. This is to be done, not by treating others as infidels, but by giving an example of what they believe in, and in being true to the example of this definition of the friends of God according to the *hadith*: "The friend of God (or the saint) is the one the sight of whom recalls God."

Now if a Muslim is called to be a witness of God, then also Muslims must know that they are not the only witnesses. For the way of Islam (both in the broader and narrower sense) is that of the search for God. It can be summed up, including its fulfilment, in these two verses: "O man, you who strive without ceasing toward your Lord, you will meet Him" (*Al Inshiqaq* 84.6), and "Wherever you turn, there is the face of God" (*Al Baqara* 2.115). In this sense, Muslims are called to see the face of God in all that surrounds them and in all human existence. Besides the *hadith* that seems to recall the gospel of Matthew (25:31ff), mentioned above, another *hadith,* associated with the ascension of the Prophet by night through the seven heavens and his encounter with God (*Mi'raj*), puts before us a dialogue between God and the Prophet. God demands of the Prophet, "At what point did you come to know Me?" The Prophet replies: "When you instructed me concerning Yourself." Then God replies, "You came to know me truly when you acted toward each one of My servants as you act toward Me."

The other, every other person, is a mirror of God. More than that, the other is the way by which we gain knowledge of God. This is because each person is a bearer of the Spirit or the Breath of God, as in the verse: "When I will have shaped him and I will have breathed into him of My Spirit, fall down and prostrate before him" (*Sad* 38.72).

Concerning Recognition

Recognition of cultural and spiritual heritage

The recognition of other religions – notably the religions of the people of the Covenant which the Qur'an addresses in the *surah, Al Ma'ida* – also includes a recognition of the Books revealed prior to Islam but belonging to the economy of the Reminder. Referred to in the Qur'an are the Torah, the Gospels, the Psalms (*Zabur*), as well as what the Qur'an calls the Pages of Abraham and of Moses, and which may correspond, according to Geneviève Gobillot, to two apocryphal testaments attributed to the two prophets: The testament and the death of Moses, found in the Book of Biblical Antiquities, and the Testament of Abraham.[9]

Thus, one of the five principles of faith of every Muslim is faith in the Books revealed by God, not just in the Qur'an. This precept may be said to contradict the thesis of the abrogation of preceding revelations by the Qur'an. Also against this thesis of abrogation, some Qur'anic verses refer to the guardians of the preceding Books, counting them as believing Muslims. Verse 7 of the *surah Al Anbiya'* (21) states: "We have only sent before you men to whom We made revelations. Ask therefore of the people of the Reminder (*ahl adh-dhikr*), if you do not know." Qur'anic commentators, including the most conservative, explain *ahl adh-dhikr* by reference to the people of the Book. The sense of this verse is supported by another, yet more specific: "If you are in doubt concerning the subject of what We have revealed to you, ask those who read the scriptures which were sent before you" (*Yunus* 10.94).

Further, the Qur'an puts forward in the *surah Al Ma'ida* a whole series of verses which describe the Old and New Testaments as guidance and light:

> In truth, We have revealed the Torah where are found a direction and a light. It is by this that the prophets who have surrendered themselves to God, the rabbis and the doctors deliver justice for the Jews, while conforming to the Book of God of which they hold the custody and of which they are witnesses. Do not fear men; fear Me! Do not sell My signs for low price. Those who do not judge according to that which God has revealed, these are the disbelievers. We have prescribed for them, in the Torah, life for life, eye for eye, nose for nose, ear for ear, tooth for tooth and, for wounds, retaliation. While concerning the one who generously refuses to exercize his right, that will be an expiation for him. Those who do not judge according to what God has revealed are wrongdoers. In the line of the prophets, We have sent Jesus, son of Mary, in order to confirm that which the Torah had imparted before him. And We have given him the Gospel in which is found a guidance and a light, confirming that which the Torah had brought and containing a guidance and a warning for those who fear God. May the people of the Gospel deliver justice according to what God has thus revealed. (*Al Ma'ida* 5.44-47)

We should note that these verses come directly before verse 48, quoted previously, which announces clearly the principle of diversity willed by God, and also calls for us to anticipate the good things which are to come, and not to lose ourselves in theological discussions when, at our return to God, it is He who will explain to us the reason or the meaning of our divergences.

It is clear that the Qur'an invites Muslims to see in these divergences a difference of interpretation of the revealed messages and not any alteration of the Books themselves. Further, it invites Muslims to recognize a common cultural and religious heritage. This is both by the fact that the Qur'an quotes the Bible and its narratives exhaustively, and by its own affirmation that it comes itself in order to confirm the scriptures. In fact, Geneviève Gobillot, quoting the verse, "This Qur'an has not been invented by any other than God, but it is that which attests the truth (*tasdiq*) of what existed before it, the explanation (*tafsil*) of the Book sent by the Lord of the universe, which does not contain any doubt"(*Yunus* 10.39), goes on to suggest that the Qur'an sees itself as a commentary on the scriptures and that it considers the people of the Book as those familiar with the scripture.[10]

From another perspective, understanding the Qur'an in the light of the scriptures, as it asks us to do, and seeing that it confirms the previous Books makes it clear that the Qur'an considers these previous books as confirming witnesses to its own veracity. In fact, the verses just quoted inviting Muslims to consult the people of the Book must be understood as inviting Muslims not only to recognize but to have knowledge of the other scriptures in order better to understand the Qur'an. The Qur'an, suggests Gabriel Said Reynolds, expects that its hearer will be familiar with the scriptures of the Jews and the Christians.[11] With the help of examples of Qur'anic narratives and their interpretation, he shows well in his work entitled *The Qur'an and Its Biblical Subtext* what one can gain from reading the Qur'an in conversation with the biblical literature that came before it. This can be more enlightening than reading it in conversation with what came after it, that is the Qur'anic exegesis, which is itself the product of a society at some distance from the time of the beginnings of Islam, and of *ulemas*, which have their own intellectual and sometimes sectarian preoccupations.[12] However, if the exegetes of the classical period, besides their own preoccupations, are somewhat diverted toward pseudo-biblical narratives, namely the *isra'iliyyat*,[13] it has not prevented some others from understanding that the Qur'an should be read in the light of the previous scriptures. Already in the 9th century CE (5th century AH), a Lebanese historian and exegete, originating from the Bekaa valley and for this reason surnamed *Al Biqa'i*,[14] explained Qur'anic verses by turning directly to the Torah, without consulting the *isra'iliyyat*, and he considered the Torah to have the same status as the *hadith*, that is, the second religious source of Islam. The 20th-century Tunisian exegete, Muhammad Tahir Ibn 'Ashur, for his part turned directly to the gospels in his Qur'anic commentary *At-Tahrir wat-Tanwir.*

This reading of the Qur'an in the light of the previous writings concerns not just the narratives but also the spiritual meaning and values held in common by the Qur'an and the scriptures. The passage of the *surah Al Ma'ida* on the scriptures as light and guidance (see above) puts the three scriptures (Torah, Gospel, and Qur'an) together in confrontation with the anti-values represented by Meccan tribal law, which seem to give precedence to the rich to the detriment of the poor and oppressed. It is clear that the judgment which the verses speak about is not a judgment according to the letter, but a weighing according to the spirit, and in accordance with the ethical vision of the scriptures. Verse 44, which mentions the Torah, states: "Those who do not judge according to what God has revealed, these are the disbelievers." Verse 57 concerning the gospel is even more explicit: "May the people of the Book render justice according to what God has there revealed. Those who do not judge according to what God has revealed are the wayward." And verse 60 sums up: "Is it the judgment of [the age of] ignorance that they seek? But who therefore is a better judge than God for people who believe assuredly?"

The Qur'an, therefore, invites both Muslims and the people of the Book to recognize these common values in their scriptures. And it gives praise to those people of the Book who recognize these values as coming from the same divine source: "Among the people of the Book, there are those who believe in God, and in what has been revealed to you and what has been revealed to them, who are humble before God, and who do not sell at low price the signs of God" (*Al Imran* 3.119), or again: "When they hear that which is revealed to the Messenger, you see their eyes fill with tears because of that which they have recognized as belonging to the Truth" (*Al Ma'ida* 5.83).

In the same way, the Muslim believer may well be moved when hearing or reading those biblical passages which recall these values, as the Sheikh of Al Azhar, Ahmed al-Tayyib, has affirmed in a television broadcast, speaking of his own experience each time he reads the Gospels, notably the Beatitudes.[15] It goes without saying that this broadcast provoked the anger of some Muslim extremists, who loudly proclaimed this "scandal" via the internet.

Finally, we see that the Qur'an itself affirms that the words of God are not limited to the Qur'an, nor even to the Books previously revealed, for it states: "Say: 'If the sea was ink for [writing] the Words of my Lord, the sea would be spent before the Words of my Lord are spent even if we replaced it with a like quantity'" (*Al Kahf* 18.109). These words of the Lord, according to the commentators on the Qur'an, are to be found not only in the totality of the scriptures but also in all creatures, each creature being a word of God according to a number of Sufi exegetes and contemporary commentators.[16]

Recognition of the authenticity of spiritual experience

As mentioned previously, the Qur'anic concept of faith is not the preserve of Muslims alone. The term *mu'umin* (believer) is used by the Qur'an to refer to those who have faith, whether they belong to the Muslim community or not. Besides, this term is not used for all Muslims, for the Qur'an distinguishes carefully among the converts to Islam between those who have faith in their hearts and those who do not: "The Bedouin say: 'We believe!' Say to them: 'You do not believe, but say rather: 'we have embraced Islam' for the faith has not yet entered you hearts" (*Al Hujurat* 49.14).

In another verse, the Qur'an distinguishes between different types of Muslims:

> We have therefore given the Book as a heritage to those of Our servants whom We have chosen. There are those among them who wrong themselves; there are those among them who hold to a middle way; and there are among them those who, with the permission

of God, overtake the others by their good works: such is the grace committed [to them]. (*Fatir* 35.32)

Thus, just as the Qur'an does not generalize in its description of the people of the Book, so it does not generalize in its description of the Muslims.

In the same way, the Qur'an takes note of the righteous among the people of the Book:

> They are not all the same: there exists among the people of the Book an upstanding community whose members recite the verses of God during the night and who make prostrations. They believe in God and in the last Day, they command that which is right and they forbid what is wrong, they compete in good works. These are part of the righteous (*salihin*). Whatever good they do, [the reward] will not be denied to them, for God knows perfectly the pious (*al muttaqin*). (*Al Imran* 3.113-115)

Elsewhere, the *surah Al Buruj,* which calls to mind the Christian martyrs of Arabia, calls them simply "the believers:" "Slain were the People of the Pit! The fire abounded in fuel while they were seated over it, witnessing what they did with the believers. They took revenge on them only because they believed in God " (*Al Buruj* 85.4-8).

Thus, in the theology of the Qur'an, the term "believer" is used for all those who have faith in God, and not just for the Muslims. This is corroborated by the research of scholar of Islam Fred Donner on the theme of faith in the Qur'an at the time of the origins of Islam. He affirms: "The line separating Believers from unbelievers did not, then, coincide simply with the boundaries of the peoples of the Book. Rather, it cut across those communities, depending on their commitment to God and to observance of His law, so that some of them were to be considered Believers, while others were not."[17]

Furthermore, according to the Qur'anic description, and as we have seen previously, faith is a journey, not an identity. It allows those who journey in faith to be gentle and open in spirit, as it permits them also to recognize whoever comes from God, and this recognition increases their own faith: "The true believers are those whose hearts quake when one mentions God. And when His signs are told, this increases their faith. And they place their confidence in their Lord" (*Al Anfal* 8.2).

Now if faith is a journey, an experience, and if it is not, theologically, the preserve of Muslims alone, it leads us to the following result: on the one hand, it is demanded of Muslims that they should recognize others' journeys of faith, and on the other, nothing prohibits a sharing of these journeys between believers of different religions.

This double position is clearly perceptible in the life of Emir Abdel Kader (d. 1883),[18] known both for his military prowess in his resistance to the French army in Algeria (1832-1847) and for his role in the saving of the lives of thousands of Christians of Damascus in 1860 from the attacks of armed groups of Muslims. But it is a third dimension of his life which interests us here, the dimension of the dialogue that throughout his life he carried on with Christians, and that intensified during his detention in France following his surrender in 1847. There he received numerous visitors, including both men and women of the religious orders, but also craftsmen and workers, men of politics, journalists, artists, and others. From his responses to his visitors, he appears not only curious to know more about the religion of others, but affirms vigorously, sometimes in the face of denial from others, that Muslims and Christians worship the same God. One of his visitors ventured: "You do not have the same God as me." Abdel Kader replied: "Our gods are not so different as you suppose; we are the children of two different mothers, but of the same father." And in confirmation of these words, he asked a nun to pray for him for, he said, "Your heart is attached only to God." This response, among others, proves his recognition of the faith of others as leading to God, and also his trust in the efficacy of their prayers.[19]

In fact the Qur'an not only recognizes the faith and works of those belonging to other religions, but it recognizes also their places of worship, as it invites not only Muslim believers but all the children of Adam to find God in every place where his adoration is proclaimed: "Say [O Muhammad]: My Lord has ordained equity. Lift up your faces toward Him in every place of prayer. Call upon him, offering him sincere worship" (*Al A'raf* 7.29). And, "O children of Adam, clothe yourselves beautifully for each place of worship" (*Al A'raf* 7.31).

The interior attitude of Abdel Kader toward others and their religion, as well as his theological position, allowed for a spiritual communion between him and a Swiss Protestant, Charles Eynard. Eynard had come to visit him with a Catholic friend, bringing him some copies of portions of the Bible, particularly the gospels, which Abdel Kader had not had access to before. After he had received his guests, he plunged into the reading of the Gospel according to St Matthew. Finishing this reading, he declared: "The religion of Jesus Christ appears to me to be more and more that of gentleness, tolerance, even the goodness of God."

This marked the beginning of a free and sincere dialogue between him and Charles Eynard which provided the basis for a lasting friendship, for it was a friendship in God. Abdel Kader refers to him in his letters as "The well-beloved in God," which calls to mind a *hadith*:

> The prophet has said: "Among the worshippers of God, there are people who are neither prophets nor martyrs, but whom the prophets and martyrs will envy at the Last Day." One asked him: "Who are they?" He replied: "These are people who are loved by the spirit of God among them, without having links of parenthood, nor goods in common. Through God their faces are alight, and they are guided by the light, they will not have fear when people are in fear, will not be afflicted when people will be afflicted [at the day of judgment]," and he quoted the Qur'an: "In truth, the well-beloved of God are sheltered from all fear, and they will never be afflicted." (*Yunus* 10.62)

Abdel Kader also calls him "the well-beloved who we have loved before the Face of God Most High" and the "one known by God" *('arif billah)*,[20] a title which one gives to the great Sufi masters.

This interreligious spiritual friendship, which is only an example among many others, proves that in an initiative of the deepening of faith, the other believer becomes a word of God. Such a friendship allows at the same time for a similar deepening in the faith of each one, a knowledge of the faith of the other, and a more profound knowledge of God, enlightened through the spiritual experience of the other.

Complementarity and Communion

"No one is ignorant of God in all his aspects..."

The spiritual experience of a follower of a particular religion does not take shape outside their religion, but at its heart. This means that when one recognizes the spiritual experience of a person of another religion, what one recognizes is at the same time part of that religion's theology.

In fact, if each religion presents a face and a conception of the divine, then reciprocal sharing and recognition of spiritual experience by the followers of different religions enables different conceptions to be seen as complementary rather than in opposition. This also allows us to be aware of the divine work outside the confines of one particular religion, widening the conception of God for whoever lives with this experience, with the constant reminder that "God is greater."

For we are talking here of an experience of sharing between believers which derives from their faith and their personal journey with the divine, and not from the arrogance of a fixed identity set up against others. And so Abdel Kader, from his experience of spiritual friendship and his lived-out theology – a man strong in his faith but humble in recognizing that the truth belongs only to God – affirms in his book of spiritual stations:

If what you think and believe is what the people of the *sunna* say, then know that He is that – and other than that. If you think and know that He is that which all the schools of Islam profess and believe – He is that and He is other than that! If you think that He is that which the various communities of faith believe – Muslims, Christians, Jews, Mazdeans, polytheists and others – He is that and He is other than that! None of his creatures worship him under all of his aspects; no-one is ignorant of Him in all his aspects.[21]

And Abdel Kader adds: "God is vast and omniscient (*Al Baqara* 2.247). He encompasses the beliefs of all creatures, just as His mercy embraces all his creatures. . . . He is the one adored by every creature from a certain perspective. He is known by all creatures from a certain perspective, and He is unknown by all creatures from a certain perspective."[22]

The anticipation of the beyond in the here-and-now

In an experience of deep faith, religions, particularly the religions of the Covenant, their Books, and their followers appear to be witnesses to one another. If one wishes to learn and to enrich oneself culturally from a shared inheritance, if one is able also to be enriched by the spiritual experience of the other, then the respective theologies also can be mutually enriching.

To give an example, the place of hope in Christian theology can present a challenge to Muslim theology in its own conception of the other world, a challenge which can only enrich its understanding. Through the idea that one is able to live the kingdom even here below, Christian theology explains the expression "anticipate the good things to come" that appears in Qur'anic verses quoted above. Now the Qur'an invites us to anticipate with one another the good things to come. Could the Qur'anic invitation mean that one may live "the beyond" in the "here-and-now" in a communion between believers of different religions who love one another in God? This is a communion of believers forming together an *umma*, literally a homogeneous community,[23] not at the level of religious identity but at the level of the degree of their faith and their witness. Believers and travellers of different belongings find themselves in a community which, after the example of Mary, is called to prostrate in worship with those who prostrate themselves (*Al Imran* 3.43), and after the example of Abraham, the friend of God, to accept in its tent all believers of good will.

To take up an image dear to Abdel Kader, human hearts will be like points in the circumference of a circle. As such, they are kindred to one another. But when they deepen their quest for the divine, they enter within the circle to find one another in its central point. There they enter into a full communion, being found in God even here below.[24]

If such is the invitation, then, in this communion, the manna received is transformed into nourishment offered to the earth, to heaven, and to the entire world. For if the apostles of Christ, according to the Qur'an, were to ask for a table, a feast, which descends from heaven to satisfy their hearts,[25] the apostles of intercommunal spiritual solidarity will offer to the heavens the fruits of the union of their hearts, satisfied within a universal fellowship.

AFTERWORDS

Fadi Daou

One easily forgets that the ownership of religious messages, at least in the monotheistic traditions, is with God. Human beings are only custodians. In consequence, religions should be ways which lead human beings out of their narrowness linked to the circumstances of their lives and their own human limits and emotions tainted by egoism, to the generosity of God – God's mercy and infinite goodness. Both the Muslim proclamation "Allahu Akbar," God is greater, and the reminder of Christ to his disciples that in his Father's house there are many rooms (cf. John 14:2) warn us against the temptation – so easy to fall into – of reducing God to the measure of our own interests, identities, and communal concerns.

If for monotheists, notably Christians and Muslims, God is unique – that is, there is only one God and he is the God of all his creatures – then the question is therefore not to know who "has" the true God, but rather who advances the most toward him and helps others in their own progress. At Assisi in 1986, John Paul II, when he was speaking of the believers of different religions, used the powerful image of "companions on the common road" that all humans are called to travel. Despite the different communities of faith that travel on it, this road cannot be other than that of the unity of human beings and of their communion with God.

In the Christian tradition, human beings are created in the image of God, and throughout their lives are called to acquire a "transparency" which allows this divine image to reveal itself in them. In other words, human life, according to the Christian faith, is a work of transfiguration by which human beings become the dwelling place of God. From this perspective, it is better to see the world not as a vale of tears but as Mount Tabor, where the light of God shines forth, illuminating humanity by God's presence. It is the wonder of divine hospitality that, in contrast to human hospitality, it is not satisfied just to welcome the other into its own space, but invites itself home to the other, so that it may be made welcome. This is an initiative which expresses deep humility, even dispossession, but which according to divine logic becomes the place of communion.

It follows that if human beings are invited to become the image of God in God's hospitality, they are also invited not only to make room for the other in their own personal or community space, but also to invite themselves home to the other, allowing themselves to be made welcome as they are, casting aside all sense of supremacy or power. For our world today, and in the dynamic of interreligious relationships, I find myself trusting that where believers allow themselves to be mutually welcomed, God is there. In writing these last lines, I have to recall yet again the monks of Tibhirine, who, in the fragility of their humanity, have become witnesses for us of this divine hospitality, and, in their unconditional gift of self to the other, a place of the epiphany of the love and glory of God.

Nayla Tabbara

One of the Names of God in Islam is *al-Wasi'*, literally "the Vast" or "the Spacious." This name is, in the Qur'an, linked both to mercy and to knowledge, and is represented by such expressions as "embracing all things" or "extending to everything" (*Al A'raf* 7.156) or "Our Lord! You embrace everything in your Mercy and in your Knowledge" (*Ghafir* 40.7).

A prophetic *hadith* instructs Muslims to "clothe themselves interiorly with the divine attributes." In a work entitled *The Ultimate Goal of the Explanation of the Most Beautiful Names of God*, the theologian Al Ghazali (d. 505 AH/111 CE) explains how the believer is able to adopt the qualities of each one of the 99 divine names. Explaining the name *al Wasi'*, he sees this as an invitation to believers to become deeper and broader in their interior life, developing their knowledge and incorporating all the ethical values.[1] Now this expansion of the interior life or "spaciousness" is not unrelated to the theme of hospitality. The name *al Wasi'*, indicating that God embraces everything through his mercy and knowledge, may be interpreted as divine hospitality. In this sense, the believing Muslim is called to cultivate hospitality in the interior life. And this hospitality has a double significance. Fundamentally, and in the first place, it is an act of faith which seeks to make space for God in the interior of one's self, in order to attain to what is promised by God in the *hadith qudsi:* "Neither my earth nor my heaven can contain me, only the heart of my believing worshipper can contain me."[2] Second, it permits the inclusion of others in the interior of the self. According to the theology of the spiritual life, it is divine love dwelling in the believer that creates a space large enough for the love and the knowledge of others to come to be contained there.

The letter of 138 Muslim scholars that was addressed in 2007 to the leaders of Christian churches and communities throughout the world, entitled *A Common Word,* makes the link between these two loves by inviting Muslim and Christian believers to unite around the two principles common to both religions: the love of God and the love of the neighbour.[3] Now the mystery of this expansion of the interior life means it is not limited to one "other" alone. Instead, because it is linked to divine hospitality, it brings about of itself an opening which, little by little, permits yet other "others" to find their place in one's interior life. For this reason, Emir Abdel Kader demands: "What greater goodness can surpass the love of the human person for humanity? If there is no love among us, do we belong to a religion in truth?... God is the God of All; and so we must love this All."[4]

Another mystery of this enlargement is that it brings about an ontological change in the self. The other is no longer external to one's own self, but the other dwells there; living out their hopes, their thoughts, and their understanding of their relationship with the world and with the divine, they become part of the self. Sheikh Jamal Rahman, a pioneer in interreligious dialogue in its spiritual dimension in the United States, states: "Harmony between religions is not possible without doing the inner work that creates the spatiousness required to embrace differences."[5]

The invitation is therefore to open in the self a breach which widens little by little, and which allows the welcoming of others "at the heart of differences": in other words, accepting these differences and taking them up, not just bypassing them. And so following the example of Abraham's welcome of the divine messengers, the hospitality required includes both sacrifice and the proclamation of fecundity. This double action of hospitality demands the sacrifice of the comfort of a cloistered existence within one's own group with its own terms of reference, not requiring contact with other groups with other terms of reference. Nevertheless, this sacrifice carries in itself the promise of the birth of a new self, capable of comprehending all beings through its internal "spaciousness" and compassion. Out of this ontological transformation there comes about a change both in approach and in action. And so "action" is no longer limited to promoting the growth of the group to which one belongs or protecting it but is turned outward toward others. If, following his hospitality shown to the messengers, Abraham took up the defence of the people of Lot, the advocates of divine hospitality are called to draw upon the resources of their own inner life in facing all obstacles and fears in their engagement for, toward, and with "the others."

Notes

1. CHRIST AND THE OTHER

1. The Samaritan schism, resulting from a reaction against the rigorism of the Jewish reform movement that followed the exile (6th century BCE), led to an implacable opposition between the two groups. A religious Jew had to avoid all contact with Samaritans, who were considered ritually unclean.

2. See: Bernard Sesboué, *Hors de l'Eglise point de salut: histoire d'une formule et problemes d'interprétation*, Desclée de Brouwer, Paris, 2004.

3. Wesley Ariarajah, *The Bible and People of Other Faiths,* Geneva, WCC Publications, 1985.

4. Christ is called "the Word" (*Logos* in Greek); it signifies that Christ is the perfect expression of the Father, the image of the invisible God and the splendour of his glory. Through the incarnation, he is the supreme manifestation of God in human form.

5. Irenaeus of Lyons, *Against Heresies,* III, 10.2.

6. Christian de Chergé was a monk, and prior of the abbey of Notre Dame de l'Atlas at Tibhirine (Algeria), who was assassinated with six of his brethren in 1996; see *Sept vies pour Dieu et l'Algérie,* Bayard/Centurion, Paris, 1996.

7. Quoted in Christian Salenson, *Christian de Chergé: une théologie de l'espérance,* Paris, Bayard, 2009, p.121.

8. Christian de Chergé, "Quand un 'a-Dieu s'envisage," in *L'invincible espérance*, Bayard/Centurion, Paris, 1997, p.223.

2. THE ECONOMY OF THE REMINDER

1. "[They speak of] the unction of God? But who, better than God, is able to give such unction? We are his worshippers!" *(Al-Baqara 2.138).*

2. Cf. Geneviève Gobillot, "*Fatara* and *Fitra*: Some Forgotten Interpretations," in *En Hommage au "Père Jacques Jomier, O.P.* (Études réunies et coordonnées par Marie-Thérèse Urvoy), Cerf, Paris, collection "Patrimoines," 2002 (p.1-120), p.111.

3. Satan.

4. "Next the Devil tempted him and said: 'O Adam, shall I show you the tree of eternity and an imperishable kingdom?' They both [Adam and Eve] ate. Then they became aware of their nakedness. They sought to cover themselves with the leaves of paradise. Adam had disobeyed his Lord and he went astray. His Lord then brought him back to Himself, accepted his repentance and guided him" (*Taha* 20.120-122).

5. "This is only a Reminder addressed to the worlds" (Sad 38.87); "This is a blessed Reminder that We have made descend. Are you then going to deny it?" (*Al-Anbiya'* 21.50; told again in *Al Hijr* 15.9).

6. The chronological order according to the classification of Noldeke-Schwally: Meccan Period, first phase: 96, 74, 111, 106, 108, 104, 107, 102, 105, 92, 94, 93, 97, 86, 91, 80, 68, 87, 95, 103, 85, 73, 101, 99, 82, 81, 53, 84, 100, 79, 77, 78, 88, 89, 75, 83, 69, 51, 52, 56, 70, 55, 112, 109, 113, 114, 1.

Meccan Period, second phase: 54, 37, 71, 76, 44, 50, 20, 26, 15, 19, 38, 36, 43, 72, 67, 23, 21, 25, 17, 27, 18.

Meccan Period, third phase: 32, 41, 45, 16, 30, 11, 14, 12, 40, 28, 29, 31, 42, 10, 34, 25, 7, 46, 6, 13.

Medinan Period: 2, 98, 64, 62, 8, 47, 3, 61, 57, 4, 65, 59, 33, 63, 24, 58, 22, 48, 66, 60, 110, 49, 9, 5.

It is necessary to add to this classification that certain verses in certain Meccan *surah*s are additions from the Medinan period, or a later phase in the same Meccan period, and certain verses in the *surah*s of the Medinan period belong to the Meccan period. [See also Richard Bell, *The Qur'an, Translated, with a Critical Re-arrangement of the Surahs*, 2 vols, Edinburgh University Press, 1937-1939.–Trans.]

7. "We have honoured the offspring of Adam, and carried them by land and by sea; We have set them upon firm earth and upon the sea, We have provided for them excellent nourishment, We have granted them a privileged place compared to many beings whom We have created" (*Al Isra'* 17.70).

8. *Hadith*: "People are equal like the teeth of a comb, no-one is superior to another except by piety."

9. "When he has turned his back [on you,] he will traverse the earth in order to sow corruption, and to destroy harvest and livestock, but God does not like corruption (*Al Baqara* 2.205)

10. Following the *hadith*: "One day when we were seated near the Messenger of God, suddenly there appeared a man dressed in garments of shining whiteness, his hair being very black, without any traces on him of a journey, a man known to none among us. He came to sit opposite the Prophet, placing his knees against his, and the palms of his hands on his thighs, he said to him: 'O Muhammad, tell me about Islam.' The Messenger of God replied: 'Islam is that you bear witness that there is no god but God and Muhammad is the Messenger of God, that you perform the prayer, pay the Zakat, fast for the month of Ramadan and make the pilgrimage to the sacred House if it is possible for you.' 'You speak truly!' said the man. We were filled with amazement to see him questioning the Prophet and approving his response. And the man asked again: 'Tell me about the subject of faith (*al-Iman*).' 'It is,' replied the Prophet, 'to believe in God, His angels, His books, His messengers, in the last day, and to believe in the destiny appointed for the good and for the evil.' 'You speak truly,' repeated the man who continued, saying, 'Inform me about right conduct (*al-Ihsan*).' 'It is', replied the Prophet, 'that you worship God as if you see Him, for if you do not see Him, surely He sees you . . . upon that the man departed. As for me I waited a moment. Then the Prophet asked me: 'O Omar, do you know who was the questioner?' I replied, 'God and his Messenger are better informed than I.' 'It is the Archangel Gabriel who has come to teach you your religion (*din*),' said the Prophet."

11. Saoud al Mawla: "Foi, raison et violence. Lecture Musulmane," in *La Théologie Politique au Service de la Paix* (under the direction of Fadi Daou) Publications de l'ISSR-USJ, Beirut, 2008 (p.67-77), p.71-72.

12. Litt. "Living, son of Awake."

13. Ahmad ibn Fares, *Mu'jam maqayis al lugha*, Beirut, Dar al Kutub al Ilmiya, 1999, vol.1, p.322.

14. According to the reading of *Ubayy* (variant in comparison with the Uthmanic Corpus), the verse said: "The religion for God is *hanifiyya*," which further supports the understanding that it refers here to Islam in the wider sense.

15. Concerning Noah, see *Yunus* 10.72: "My reward is from God alone, and I have received the order to be of those who submit themselves to Him [*Muslimun*]." For Joseph, son of Jacob, see 12.101: "O my Lord! You have invested me with sovereignty and you have taught me the interpretation of events. Creator of the heavens and the earth, you are my Protector in this world and in the other. Grant that I may die as one who submits to You [*Muslim*] and place me among the righteous!" For the apostles, see *Al Imran* 3.52: "When he has noticed their disbelief, Jesus said: 'Who are my helpers in the way of God?' The apostles said: 'We are the helpers of God; we believe in God; witness that we are those who submit themselves [*Muslimun*]!'"; for the people of Moses, see *Yunus* 10.84: "Moses said: 'O my people! If you believe in God, return to Him if you are submitted to Him [*Muslimin*]'; . . . Moses and Aaron spoke to Pharoah: 'You wish to take revenge on us simply because we have believed the signs of our Lord when they came to us.' Lord! Grant us patience and let us die in a state of submission!" (*Al A'raf* 7.126). Jacob and his sons: "Were you witnesses, when death came to Jacob and he said to his sons: 'Who are you going to worship after me?' They said: 'We will worship your God and the God of your fathers: Abraham, Ishmael and Isaac, a unique God! And to him we will be submissive [*Muslimin*]!'" (*Al Baqara* 2.133). Solomon and the queen of Sheba: "She said: 'My Lord! I have wronged myself, and I submit with Solomon to God, Lord of the worlds!'" (*An-Naml* 27.44)

3. COVENANTS AND REVELATIONS

1. Jezreel, Lo-ruhamah, and Lo-ammi are the names of the children of Hosea, born from prostitution. Etymologically, *Jezreel* means, "God sows"; *Lo-ruhamah,* "Unloved"; and *Lo-Ammi,* "Not my people."

2. Irenaeus of Lyons, *Against Heresies*, III, 12, 13.

3. Jean Daniélou, *Les Saints "paiens" dans l'Ancien Testament*, Seuil, Paris, 1956, p.33.

4. Cf. Jacques Dupuis, *Vers une theologie chretienne du pluralisme religieux,* Cerf, Paris, 1999, p.54-75.

5. John Paul II, *Encyclical Letter Slavorum Apostoli*, 1985, no.19.

6. J. Dupuis, *op. cit.*, p.350.

7. Ibid., 353.

8. The Council of the Catholic Patriarchs of the East, *Ensemble devant Dieu pour le bien de l'homme et de la* société, 1994, no.44, p.72.

9. Christian de Chergé, "Quand un `a-Dieu s'envisage," in *L'invincible espérance*, Bayard/Centurion, Paris, 1997, p.113.

10. Ibid., p.171.

11. Ibid., p.112.

12. Michel Hayek, *Le Mystere d'Ismael*, Paris, Mame, 1964, p.194.

13. Ibid., p.239.

14. Ibid., p.224.

15. Ibid., p.197.

16. Ibid., p.197.

17. Ibid., p.200.

18. Ibid., p.241.

19. In Muslim tradition this source is named "Zamzam," cf. Ibn Kathir, *Qasas Al-Anbiya'*, p.156.

20. Cf. *Saint Ephraem, Hymni et sermones*, edited by T.J Lamy, t.1, 83; as quoted in Michel Hayek, *op. cit.*, p.231.

21. Ibid., p.247.

22. Youakim Moubarac, *Abraham dans le Coran*, Vrin, Paris, 1958.

23. Ibid., p.100.

24. Ibid., p 71.

25. Youakim Moubarac, *Pentalogie islamo-chrétienne: L'Islam et le dialogue islamo-chrétien*, vol.3, edited by Cénacle Libanais, Beyrouth, 1972, p.111-112.

26. Mouchir Basile Aoun, "Le dialogue islamo-chrétien comme 'lieu' théologique," in Youakim Moubarac, *Les Dossiers H*, Lausanne, 2005, p.204.

27. Claude Geffré, *De Babel à la Pentecote: Essais de théologie interreligieuse*, Cerf, Paris, "Cogitatio fidei" 247, 2006, p.180.

28. Ibid., p.170.

29. René Habachi, *Orient quel est ton Occident?* Centurion, Paris, 1969, p.36.

30. Christian de Chergé, *L'invincible espérance, op. cit.*, p.111.

31. GRIC, *Ces Écritures qui nous questionnent*, Centurion, Paris, 1987, p.134.

32. R.C. Zaehner, *Concordant Discord*, Clarendon Press, Oxford, 1970, cited in J.Dupuis, *op. cit.*, p.373.

33. J. Dupuis, *op.cit.*, p.373.

34. Congregation for the Doctrine of the Faith, *The Declaration "Dominus Iesus": On the Unicity and Salvific Universality of Jesus Christ and the Church*, Vatican City, 2000, section 8.

35. Cf. Nasr Hamed Abou Zaid, *Le concept du texte: étude des sciences coraniques* (in Arabic), Beyrouth, *Al-markaz al-thalqafi al-arabi*, 2011.

36. J. Dupuis, *op. cit.*, p.379.

37. International Theological Commission, "Christianity and the World Religions," para.91., http://www.vatican.va/roman_curia/congregations/cfaith/cti_documents/rc_cti_20120308_ladaria_en.html.

38. Georges Khodr, "The Christians of the Orient in a Pluralist Context," in *Juifs, Chrétiens, Musulmans: que pensent les uns des autres?* Labor et fides, Geneva, 2004, p.67.

39. *Idem.*

40. Joseph Doré, "*La presence du Christ dans les religions non-chrétiennes*," in *Chemins de dialogue* 9 (1997), p.48

41. John Paul II, "The World Situation and the Spirit of Assisi," Discourse to the Cardinals and the Curia," 22 December 1986, section 5. [*Documentation Catholique*, no. 1933, p.134].

42. Ibid., section 3, p.133.

43. John Paul II, *Redemptoris Missio: On the Permanent Validity of the Church's Missionary Mandate*, Vatican City, 1990, no.15.

44. John Paul II, "The World Situation and the Spirit of Assisi," *op. cit.*, no.7, p 134. (Author's translation from the French.)

45. Retreat preached for the Little Sisters of Jesus in Morocco in 1990; cited in Christian Salenson, *Christian de Chergé: une théologie de l'espérance*, Bayard, 2009, Paris, p.194.

4. ISLAM AND OTHER RELIGIONS

1. *Al Baqara* 2.62; *Al Ma'ida* 5.69.

2. *Al Hajj* 22.17.

3. Cf. Geneviève Gobillot, "La demonstration de l'existence de Dieu comme élément du caractère sacré d'un texte: De hellénisme tardif au Coran," in *Al Kitab: La sacralité du texte dans le monde de l'Islam*, edited by D. de Smet, G. de Callatay, and J.M.F van Reeth, Louvain-la-Neuve, 2004, p.103-142.

4. "Have you considered al-Lat and al-'Uzza, and the other, Manat, the third?" (*An-Najm* 53.19-20).

5. "They have assigned to God as associates the *jinn,* when it is He who has created them; and, without knowing anything, they falsely assign to him sons and daughters. Glory be to Him, and may he be exalted above that which they attribute (to Him)!" (*An An'am* 6.100); or again, "Has your Lord reserved for you male children and taken (for Himself) daughters from among the angels?" (*Al Isra* 17.40).

6. "We brought the children of Israel across the sea. Pharaoh and his armies chased them relentlessly with rage until, at the point of being drowned, Pharaoh cried out: 'I believe that there is no god but Him in whom the children of Israel believe, and I join myself to those who submit themselves to Him'" (*Yunus* 10.90).

7. "They are nothing but names that you and your fathers have named, without God having given them any power whatsoever. They only follow some conjectures and what drives their souls, even though the Guidance of their Lord has come to them" (*An-Najm* 53.23).

8. Hud said: "The condemnation and the anger of your Lord have fallen upon you! Would you dispute with me about names that you and your fathers have named concerning whom God has given no power? Wait therefore! For I shall stay waiting with you!" (*Al A'raf* 7.71).

9. "Have you not considered the case of the one to whom God had given kingship and who made a dispute with Abraham on the subject of his Lord? Abraham had said, "My Lord is He who grants life and deals death." Abraham spoke to him again: "God makes the sun come from the East; make it then rise from the West!" He who had disbelieved was then confounded. God does not guide the evil-doers" (*Al Baqara* 2.258); "[Remember the day where] Abraham said to his father Azar: 'Do you take idols for gods? I see you, you and your people, as clearly in error'" (*Al-An'am* 6.74).

10. Aziz Esmail,"Philosophical Remarks on Scripture," in *Al Kitab, op. cit.,* p.41.

11. "They say: 'Burn him! And help your gods, if you are able!' We decreed: 'O fire! Be for Abraham refreshment and peace!' They wished to trick him but We have made them the most miserable of losers"(*Al Anbiya'* 21.68-70).

12. The rigorist commentators explain "The religion for God is Islam" (3.19) as meaning Islam in the more restricted sense. They take these verses to affirm salvation for the adherents of other monotheistic religions, as meaningless once Islam started. According to them, Jews, Christians and

Sabians who lived before the coming of Islam will receive salvation, but not those who remain followers of those religions after the appearance of Islam.

13. Tabari, *Tafsir at-Tabari (Al Musamma Jami'al Bayan fi tafsir la Qur'an)*, Dar al Kutub al Ilmiyya, Beirut, 1999, I:410-412.

14. Abdelmajid Charfi, *La penséé islamique, rupture et fidelité*, Albin Michel, Paris, 2008, p.193-194.

15. "Remember: 'We have made the House a place of gathering and of rest for human beings, enjoining them to take the station of Abraham as an area for prayer. We concluded a pact with Abraham and Ishmael in order that they would purify my House for those who carry out the circuits there, and make a devotional retreat, bending and prostrating themselves'" *(Al Baqara* 2.125).

16. Cf. Massignon, *La Mubhalah de Médine et l'hyperdulie de Fatima*, in *Opera Minora*, Dar al Ma'aref, Liban,1963, 1:551-572.

17. While this pact of Medina is taken from the *sira*, which is at least a century and a half later than the beginning of Islam, Fred Donner affirms that the text is so different in what it contains and in its style from all the other texts in the collections of *sira* that it is accepted as authentic by all researchers on the origins of Islam, even the most sceptical among them.

18. Ibn Hisham, *As-Sira an Nabawiyya*, Dar al Kutub al Ilmiyya, Beirut, 2009, vol.2, p.86.

19. Tribute that the Christians, Jews, and followers of other religions regarded as religions of the Book by Muslims had to pay, during all the period of Islamic rule.

20. Notably the different versions of the *sira*, which we have to remember were not written until the end of the second half of the second century of the Hijra (8th century CE).

21. *Dhimmitude* or *of dhimma*, that is, being *dhimmi*, under Omayyad, Abbasid, and Mamluk rule, as well as for a major part of the Ottoman reign, and under the rule of other local dynasties in the Muslim world in the medieval period. This status allowed a certain freedom of worship but not of conscience, requiring the payment of a tax. Further, the people of the Book were not allowed to be full citizens because they were not permitted to join the army. During some periods this law regarding the *dhimmi* was manifested in a relative tolerance, while at other times it resulted in

discrimination: in some periods, for example, the *dhimmis* had to wear clothes or accessories distinguishing them from Muslims.

22. Historical research has not yet found evidence of the possible existence of a Christian community in Arabia in the 7th century CE that transformed the Trinity into such a triad.

23. The accounts concerning Uzayr in the histories of the prophets correspond sometimes to Ezra and sometimes to Isaiah (cf. Ibn Kathir, Tafsir, commentary on *surah* 9.30, and Ibn Kathir, *Qasas al Anbiya'*, p.523-537).

According to Michel Hayek, however, he is not to be identified with Ezra but with Ozael, the name given in rabbinic literature to the "sons of God" who had contracted marriage with the daughters of men, Gen. 6:1-4. (See Michel Hayek, *Le Mystère d'Ismael*, Mame, Paris, 1964, p.79-80.)

24. Tabari, *op. cit.*, III., p.289.

25. See http://www.altafsir.com/Tafasir.asp?tMadhNo=0%tTafsirNo= 54&tSoraNo=3&tAyahNo=55&tDisplay=yes&Page=2&Size1&Languageg eld=1

26. Ibn Hisham, *As-Sira an Nabawiyya, op. cit.*, vol.4, p.35.

27. The last *surah* contains the last words of the revelation in its third verse: "Today, I have completed your Religion, I have accomplished My blessing upon you, and I have approved Islam to be your Religion" (*Al Ma'ida* 5.3).

28. "Why do the rabbis and doctors (of the religious Law) not prevent them from using lying words, and eating from unlawful gains? How bad are their deeds!" (*Al Ma'ida* 5.63).

29. *Al Ma'ida* 5.17.

30. Abdul Karim Soroush, *The Straight Paths* (in Arabic: *As-Siratat al mstaqima*), trans. Ahmad Alqabanji, Dar al Intishar al 'Arabi, Beirut, 2009, p.52.

31. See *Al Ma'ida* 2.62.

32. Mahmoud Ayoub,"Religious Pluralism in the Qur'an," in *Mutual Perceptions between Christians and Muslims Past and Present* (in Arabic: *An-Nadharat al Mutabadala bayna al Masihiyyin wal Muslimin fil Madi wal Hadir*), Balamand University, Lebanon, 1997, p.24.

33. As the verse indicates: "He has created you and you will be brought back to life as a one single soul" (*Luqman* 31.28).

34. Soroush, *op. cit.*, p.49.

35. Ahmad Ibn Fares (d. 395H / 1005CE), *Mu'jam maqayis al-lugha*, Dar al Kutub al 'Ilmiyya, Beirut, 1999, vol.2, p.343.

36. Daniel Madigan, *The Qur'an's Self Image*, Princeton, 2001, p.165.

37. Cf. *Lisan al Arab*.

38. Farid Esack, *Qur'an, Liberation and Pluralism*, Oneworld Publications, Oxford, 1997 [2002], p.153.

39. Abu Yusuf Ya'qub, *Kitab al Kharaj*, Freiburg, Al Kamel Verlag, 2009.

40. Shahrastani (d. 548H / 1153CE), *Al Milal wan-Nihal*, Dar al Ma'rifa, Beirut, 2001.

41. Hayek, *op. cit.*, p.193.

42. Speaking of faith, the Qur'an states: "Whoever believes in God, God guides his heart. God is Omniscient" (*At Taghabun* 64.11); "O you who believe! Respond to God and to the Messenger when he calls you to that which will give you true life, and know that God interposes between a man and his heart, and that it is to Him that you will be gathered" (*Al Anfal* 8.24); "He has placed faith in their hearts and He has aided them with His support" (*Al Muhadala* 58.22). Speaking of disbelief, it also states: "It is thus that We make enter [disbelief] into the heart of the guilty ones" (*Al Hijr* 15.12).

43. Esack, *op. cit.*, pp.117-25 and pp. 134-44.

5. THE CHURCH AND OTHER RELIGIONS

1. John Paul II, *Redemptoris Missio: On the Permanent Validity of the Church's Missionary Mandate*, Vatican City, 1990, no.55.

2. Congregation for the Doctrine of the Faith, *The Declaration "Dominus Iesus": On the Unicity and Salvific Universality of Jesus Christ and the Church*, Vatican City, 2000, para.21.

3. John Paul II, "The World Situation and the Spirit of Assisi," Discourse to the Cardinals and the Curia," 22 December 1986, p.60 [*Documentation Catholique*, no. 1933].

4. Cf. Joseph Doré, "*La presence du Christ dans les religions non-chrétiennes*," in *Chemins de dialogue* 9 (1997), p.39.

5. Council of Catholic Patriarchs of the East, *Ensemble devant Dieu pour le bien de l'homme et de la* société, 1994, no.44.

6. See: Joseph Ratzinger, "Le relativisme est aujourd'hui le problème central de la foi et de la théologie," *Documentation Catholique*, no. 2151 (1997), p.29-37.

7. Ibid., p.30.

8. Cf. Ibid., p.31.

9. Referred to in Guyonne de Montjou, *Mar Moussa, Un monastere, un homme, un desert,* Paris Albin Michel, 2006, p.197. Pere Paolo Dall'Oglio is the founder of the Community Al-Khalil (the Arabic title of Abraham), at the monastery of St Moses the Ethiopian in Syria. The principal charism of the community is to be witnesses of the love which Christ has for Islam and Muslims. For more information, see: www.deirmarmusa.org.

10. Paul VI, *Evangelii nuntiandi,* Vatican City, 1975, no.5.

11. Benedict XVI, "Homily at the Inauguration of the Pontificate" (24 April 2005).

12. Benedict XVI, "Discourse on the Occasion of the Fortieth Anniversary of the Decree *Ad gentes,*" 11 March 2006.

13. Congregation for the Doctrine of the Faith, "Doctrinal Note on Certain Aspects of Evangelisation," 3 December 2007.

14. Cf. ibid., no.3.

15. Cf. ibid., no.9.

16. Christian Salenson, *Christian de Chergé: une théologie de l'espérance,* Paris, Bayard, 2009, p.195.

17. Quoted in *Dialogue and Proclamation* 79.

18. International Theological Commission, "Christianity and the World Religions," no.103. [Author's translation.]

19. Ibid., no.107.

20. Bartholomew I, "The Necessity of Interreligious Dialogue in the Modern World," Discourse on the occasion of obtaining the title of doctor honoris causa at the Catholic University of John Paul ll, Lublin, Poland, 20 August 2010.

21. See: www.dimmid.eu; Pierre-Francois de Béthune, *Par la foi et l'hospitalité. Essais sur la rencontre entre les religions,* Cahiers de Clerlande, no.4, Publication de Saint-André, Ottignies, 1997.

22. www.dimmid.eu/ Rubrique: "les sessions"; 9 September 2010.

23. Quoted in Montjou, *op. cit.,* p.29.

24. Council of Catholic Patriarchs of the East, *Ensemble devant Dieu, op.cit.,* no.44.

25. Christian Salenson, *Christian de Chergé: une théologie de l'espérance,* Bayard, Paris,2009, p.165.

6. RECOGNITION AND COMMUNION

1. Mahmoud Ayoub, *"Al Kawniyya, ash-shumuliyya wat-ta'addudiyya fil masihiyya wal islam,"* in *Ad-Din wal 'awlama wat-ta-'addudiyya* (Religon, globalisation and plurality), Balamand, 2000 (p.51-64), p.55.

2. Tabar Tabari, *Tafsir at-Tabari (Al Musamma Jami'al Bayan fi tafsir la qur'an)*, Dar al Kutub al Ilmiyya, Beirut, 1999, I:361-65.

3. Ayoub, "Al Kawniyya," *op. cit.*, p.58.

4. Abdelmajid Charfi, *La pensée islamique, rupture et fidelité*, Albin Michel, Paris, 2008, p.217.

5. Hallaj, *Diwan*, Al Kamel Verlag, Cologne/Beirut/Baghdad,1997, p.60.

6. Hmida Ennaifer, "An nubuwwa wal 'alam, 'alamiyyat al khususiyya fil khitab al qur'ani," in *Ad-Din wal'awlama wat-ta'addudiyya*, Balamand, 2000 (p.65-84), p.77-80.

7. Makram Mohammad Ahmad: "Interview en profondeur avec le cheikh d'Al Azhar," in the review *Al Kashkoul* (no.13/114, August–September 2010), p.44.

8. "God has taken Abraham as a friend" *(An-Nisa' 4.125)*.

9. Geneviève Gobillot, "Le Coran, le commentaire des écritures," in *Chrétiens face à l'islam*, Bayard, Paris,2009, p.163.

10. Ibid.

11. Gabriel Said Reynolds, *The Qur'an and Its Biblical Subtext*, Routledge, Abingdon, 2010, p.2.

12. Ibid., p.13 and p.22.

13. Narratives used by commentators in order to explain the Qur'anic narratives and which are an echo of the biblical narratives, except that these *Isra'iliyyat* are not rooted in the scriptures but in oral tradition and are for the most part false accounts attributed to converts of the first period of Islam, such as Ka'b al Ahbar and Wahb ibn Munabbih.

14. Ibrahim Ibn 'Umar al Biqa'i (d. 885 AH / 1480 CE), author among others of *Nazm ad-durar fi tanasub al 'ayat was-suwar*, known under the name of Tafsir al Biqa'i, also of *Masa'id an-Nazar lil ishraf 'ala maqasid as-suwar*.

15. http://www.youtube.com/watch?v=ubbdskcXaHI&feature=relatedh ttp://www.youtube.com/watch?v=ubbdskcXaHI&feature=related

16. Cf. Nayla Tabbara, *"La Parole de Dieu dans l'exégèse coranique: du particulier à l'universel,"* in Écritures et Traditions: *Diversité des lectures*, edited by Fadi Daou, Beirut, Publications of the ISSR-USJ, 2008, p.107-22.

17. Fred Donner, *Muhammad and the Believers: At the Origins of Islam*, Harvard University Press, Cambridge, p.70.

18. Emil Abdel Kader was born in Algeria in 1808 to a family of the *tariqa Qadiriyya* (one of the Sufi orders), his father holding responsibility for the *tariqa* in Algeria. Following the French invasion of Algeria in 1830, he was proclaimed Emir of the Jihad in 1832. Until his surrender in 1847, he struck the imagination of his compatriots and adversaries through his asceticism, self-discipline, behaviour and bravery. Following his surrender, he was guarded by a number of Algerians who surrendered with him and remained under detention in France until their liberation by Napoleon III in the autumn of 1852, who gave Kader permission to return to the Orient but not to Algeria. He lived until 1855 in Turkey, then Damascus, where he died in 1883. There he played a very important role in the events of 1860. Realizing that the battles between the Druze and Christians of Mount Lebanon were going to extend to Syria, he wrote to the Turkish governors and Muslim religious leaders asking them to restrain the men of their communities, while he wrote to the European representatives to warn them of the imminent danger. But the attacks took place in July 1860 and 3000 Christians were killed. Placing himself at the heart of the Christian quarter of Damascus, he succeeded, with the Algerian cavalry with him, in saving around 6000 Christians, giving them refuge in his house and then in the citadel of Damascus.

19. Cf. Ahmed Bouyerdene, *Abdel Kader l'harmonie des contraires*, Seuil, Paris,2008, p.142-146.

20. Ibid., p.204-206.

21. Abdel Kader al Jaza'iri, *Al Mawaqif ar-Ruhiyya wal Fuyudat al Sufi-yya*, Dar al Kutub al 'Ilmiyya, Beirut, 2004, vol.2, p.20-22; *Mawqif* 254.

22. Ibid., p.22.

23. We note that the term *umma*, which is today used to signify the Muslim community – whether religious, socio-political or even virtual – only appears one time in the Qur'an with the adjective Muslim attached to it, and that in a prayer of Abraham asking God to make of his descendants a homogenous group submitted to God *(Al Baqqara* 2.127-128). Otherwise, the Qur'an uses the term *umma* to signify any homogenous group, and not just a community with the same religious identity (see for example *Al An'am* 6.38 and *Al 'Imran* 3.104).

24. Cf. Bouyerdene, *op. cit.,* p.216.

25. Qur'an, *Al Ma'ida* 5.112-113.

AFTERWORDS

1. Abu Hamid al Ghazali, *Al Maqsad al Asna fi harh Asma' Allah al Husna,* Dar al Kutub al Ilmiyya, Beirut, 2001, p.146-47.

2. N.B.: Where God speaks in the first person.

3. See *A Common Word* website: http://www.acommonword.com.

4. Cf. Ahmed Bouyerdene, *Abdel Kader l'harmonie des contraires,* Seuil, Paris, 2008, p.216.

5. Don Mackenzie, Rabbi Ted Falcon, and Sheikh Jamal Rahman, *Getting to the Heart of Interfaith,* Skylight Paths, Vermont, 2010, p.40.